TABLE OF CONTENTS

Introduction 1

Chapter 1: Spiritual Transformation 3

Chapter 2: Spirituality Understood 18

Chapter 3: How To Raise Your Consciousness 25

Chapter 4: Spiritual Awakening 34

Chapter 5: The Spiritual Elements 45

Chapter 6: Six fundamental principles in spiritual practice 55

Chapter 7: You Can Achieve The Impossible 69

Chapter 8: The Souled Being Within 79

Chapter 9: The Beauty Of Compassion 90

Chapter 10: Spiritual Healing 98

Chapter 11: Chakra Cleansing and Healing 111

Chapter 12: Prayer and Peace 125

Introduction

Do you find yourself asking many questions pertaining to spirituality? Do you find yourself yearning more out of life? The spiritual transformation can help you with answering all of those questions and much more. You will gain valuable insight into many varying spiritual concepts and beliefs and learn about what spirituality represents within the body, soul, and spirit. There are concepts regarding compassion, peace, prayer, and joy as well as achievements regarding doing what is best for our own selves as life lessons we can learn from.

The spiritual transformation will allow you to awaken spiritually, and transform yourself from a spiritual amateur to someone who understands greater spiritual concepts and understandings. It is of extreme importance that you understand the many processes that occur when a person is undergoing a spiritual awakening. The concept of spirituality is a complex one and has many facets and understandings to it and you'll need guidance when it comes to this topic regarding the soul, love, light and many spiritual concepts that do occur within a person's body, mind and stages of life.

Spirituality is the key to understanding ourselves, our lives and greater and more substantial aspects of our worlds. We are spiritual beings and individuals living in a world of the material and physical yet experiencing aspects through the lens of common and basic spirituality notions and ideations. Without spirituality or spiritual awakening we're stuck and remain stagnant in a world full of the physical only so it's important to delve into spiritual concepts and ask many important questions and learn more about the spiritual world.

Transformation takes place when we reach heightened states of beauty and awareness, and our bodies and souls are ready to begin to take the next steps towards awakening and towards the path to enlightenment. There are many various elements within the concept of spirituality and it's important to learn and understand who we are spiritually and how to better ourselves and become better people overall. The spiritual transformation is one where the end of physicality exists and something new and greater begins to yield and move forward.

Chapter 1

Spiritual Transformation

Do you strive to be a spiritual person? Do you feel spirituality is something you can achieve on your own or do you feel it's something that comes to you naturally? Spirituality is a gracious and amazing part of our soul and is something we should always strive to continue to grow within our own beautiful selves. We are spiritually souled amazing beings living beautiful fulfilling lives in our own spaces within the confines of our own worlds and realms. The spiritual transformation is a place you'll want to be when you finally take the leap towards a higher consciousness and growing and expanding your awareness and your capable beautiful mind.

The spiritual transformation is one where we find ourselves wanting and yearning for that which we so desired which is our own spiritual selves and journey. Do you strive to spiritually transform yourselves and elevate your consciousness and your ways of thinking? Do you feel that this is going to help you achieve a more balanced way of life and thinking?

Spiritual transformation is one of the most beautiful facets that a person can undergo when they spiritually awaken. Transformation takes place when a souled person undergoes a transition within, and they spiritually awaken to their higher selves or to their souls and go through a magnificent and forceful transformation within their physical, and spiritual bodies.

Spiritual beauty that we find in ourselves our own souls, and all the wonderful elements we are, or which we can express, is going to be taught by our own inner selves in order to gain a greater understanding of what true spirituality is. Compassion is the key to living a beautiful fruitful life within the harmony that is present in ourselves.

Compassion is the key and gateway to living a more abundant spiritual life and a better life in general. It allows us to find the witness sympathy for those scenarios and situations that need be and allows us to hold a greater understanding and awareness or care for everyone and everything around us. We should all live our lives with a clean slate of compassion for each and every task that we partake in, for compassion is the fundamental key to understanding our own souls, and other people's trials and tribulations and the means for us to grow spiritually and internally in a great and beautiful way.

It allows us to understand other people's situations with great empathy and allows us to become extremely beautiful people full of extreme love and positivity, and to understand every situation with the lens of love, light, and extreme empathy. Empathy is one of the keys to compassion and love, and for a person to transform themselves into harmonious, wonderful, spiritual beings full of love and joy, who understand other people's situations, who possess the utmost sympathy and caring for others and for nature and animals, and who care about each and every living being as it was their own self. This is the reason compassion is one of the most important keys to love, light, and complete spiritual transformation on this plane of existence.

We are spiritual beings living in a world of materialism and in a place where we feel the spiritual elements have been lost and yet we still seek to attain the spirituality that is deep within us. We often live in a land of confusion and angst, rather than positivity and harmony, and need to revert back to seeking those elements of goodness, love, peace, and harmony in order to become greater spiritual beings in the collective masses of our own selves and our communities, lives, and on this planet.

I am a spiritual being and a light worker. I live in a reality where I seek to obtain the light that is within me and where I try to encourage more of that which is love and of the light rather than negativity harrowing and anything of the darkness. I seek to do only good and promote that which is good and beneficial for the gain and benefit of each other, and everyone as a whole, and not just for myself.

I am a multi-faceted creation of all that is within me. I have found many different elements within myself and have discovered the beauty and nature that constitutes the gift that is light and love and all of the wonders they bring forth.

Most of us are in need of repeating mantras similar to this one in order to gain a greater understanding and appreciation of all that we are and what we're capable of accomplishing as spirited light workers and light beings here on this planet to do good deeds and spread harmony to others.

Spirituality is the essence of our souls. It is the most beautiful facet that we have to experience in our holy great world, and it is one of the few key elements that we find within ourselves and trying to better our own lives in reality and bring more peace and harmony within our wonderful lives. Within the lives that we live we bring about disharmony to ourselves very often, and must focus only on that which is harmonious, and beneficial in order to bring only positive benefit to ourselves and those around us.

I am a spiritual being deep within myself and I find myself basking in the glory of being able to find my own soul and the light within me and the many beautiful areas that I can spread my goodness to. Spirituality is the key element to grasp in order to gain access to the higher dimensions and for you to gain a greater awareness of understanding and knowledge of those around you and of yourselves.

Have you ever wondered what it was like to live a life of beauty and fulfillment? Have you wanted to live a greater life full of beautiful abundance and blessings- you can find and live that life through the key elements of spirituality, and by transforming yourself from a random human created only of materialistic quality, to that of a full light being, submerged in heavenly and holy light energy from the higher dimensions. This is the spiritual transformation we are hoping to partake in and undergo. We strive to undergo the spiritual transformation in all of its glory and great presence and turn into humbled, and wondrous great light beings who are fully submerged only in love and light here on this planet to spread that which is heavenly and good, and eliminate all that is negative and unholy.

We seek that which we cannot grasp or know. We're constantly looking for ways to find beauty and love within the confines of our own limited lives and experiences. Have you always wanted to be a spiritual person, or do you feel you're at a level where you're ready for a transformation to take place?

I believe in all spiritual aspects with regards to myself and my own beliefs and practices and feel that with whatever I do there is great intent to do gracious wonderful things and only with the concept and idea that I am a fully whole spiritual creation here to do amazing work for the planet and so help others and the world.

The spiritual transformation is the key and gateway to turning into humbled great spiritual beings and lightworkers who live on this planet to do great work and to humble ourselves to the planet and to God and all that is wondrous nature in its beauty and glory.

We must transform ourselves from being physically souled creatures, into gracious, loving, kind, spiritual beings who live our lives only to do great work and harmony whose sole purpose is to better the planet and better the world for ourselves, our loved ones and for humanity as a whole and all of nature and all of the wonderful animals that exist within it.

Spirituality is the beauty that we hold the love and light that we accept within ourselves of our glory, and what radiates our souls in the passions that exist within us we are spiritual beings, living, multifaceted, beautiful lives, which we find heartwarming and contagious. We find ourselves isolated from all the things that we desire and that we love.

How can we be more spiritual?

We are in a wonderful spiritual state of harmony on this planet. In order to be more spiritual, we must focus on harmony, love, joy, and begin by practicing these beliefs more and openly in order to further become more spiritual harmonious human beings.

Another feat we can accomplish is practicing goodness and positivity and living lives full of beneficial states and living with very good intent. We must partake in every action with the best of intentions and only with these and this is one way we can become more spiritual, harmonious people.

We can practice by becoming better people overall, and raising our awareness and consciousness overall, and learning to understand our own actions and beliefs and how they relate to us and to others. We can also benefit from increasing our love within and practicing and preaching this state of love to others. This is another way to become more spiritual. Prayer and fasting or meditation are also key ways of becoming more spiritual people. It's extremely important to pray constantly to your Creator and to focus on prayers and focus on goodness and be in a constant state of meditation in order to achieve divine love and goodness, and a huge increase of spirituality in our lives.

There are many elements and areas of spirituality that most of us have not yet attained yet seek to understand in a greater form. We just know that we want to learn more and strive to be a part of something greater than our own selves. Spirituality is a vast topic and one that most people have fully yet to understand and grasp.

How does one become a more spiritual person and awaken and grow and yearn to achieve to be a greater part of other than being their normal human self? This is one important question that many people might ask themselves if they're striving to be of a higher spiritual understanding and within the nature of the spiritual being they truly are meant to be. We are not just regular human living random lives on this planet.

We are part of a greater whole out there. You might feel that you are a human being but there is simply more to you than just a regular human body. That of course, isn't just the soul, but there are many elements involved other than just the soul that exist within or that are a greater part of our wonderful spiritual selves. There are many parts that make up part of the spiritual self within us. Now what is the spiritual self? The spiritual self is the part of us that makes up the non-physical part of our bodies or our make-up and that which isn't just the regular material part that our bodies are.

Some parts that make up our spiritual body include the essence of our soul being and our higher self. Now what Is the essence of our soul being? The essence of our soul being is the greater part of ourselves and of our soul. It is the part of us that consists of the souled being in the higher vibrational areas and this is primarily what our spiritual self consists of- the higher part of our soul or the part that exists in the higher planes that is consistent or harmonious with God or God's energy. It is the part of us that exists that is in direct connection with God and the higher planes and realms. This part of our soul and being is key in developing our own spiritual natures and in becoming greater and more enlightened beings and assists with helping grow ourselves and expand our spiritual awareness in it's greatness and entirety.

The other part of our spiritual selves consists of our higher self, which is the part of ourself that consists of us that is in direct connection with the higher dimensions and planes and even with God. This part of ourselves is an extremely important part of our spiritual body and make up. The spiritual body is our connection to energy and to our higher selves and the higher dimensions. The spiritual body as described in many religious texts including the Bible or the Quran is the part of the body that doesn't undergo any form of disease or problems, like the mortal, material body does.

Four Parts Of The Body

Some believe that the body consists of four parts- physical, mental, emotional and spiritual. Jill Willard, an intuitive teaches this very concept. She feels the body consists of four very important parts.

The Physical Body

The Physical part of the body represents our skin and everything under the skin, the brain, the organs, and everything between the ears. It is the skeletal system, fascia, organs, and blood, veins, and ligaments. We usually know when our physical body is full or not, hurt or not, happy or not, healthy or not. The signs are very well-known to us. Medical practices and the western culture way of thinking, places a lot of emphasis on this body and tries to ensure that it doesn't experience a lot of pain or discomfort, and uses methods to ease any kind of issues or pain associated with this body.

When this part of our body is balanced, we should feel open, flexible and healthful, our vitamin and mineral elements should be balanced, and we should be free of pain, toxicity, and acidity, and have minimal health issues and live happy, balanced, healthy lives overall and in general. When the body isn't balanced, then there are a host of health issues, cells and body parts breaking down easily, a whole host of health issues and other aspects that occur within the body. There are specific ways of making sure that this portion of the body stays in harmony and balance which include simple movements and slow, balanced repetitive sequences, meditation, walking, massage, barefoot or bare hand earth play, yoga, stretching, and weight bearing exercises that let you feel the strength in your own body and the union of all things physical.

The Emotional Body

The Emotional body is the second part of the body that Jill Willard believes exists as being a part of the body and it includes the nervous system, hormones, touch, water and water release (tears), and water absorption. Some believe that the emotional body extends a few millimeters or inches around the body. How we are doing emotionally is represented by how calm or rough the waters are in our thoughts and our dream state.

When balanced, the emotional body should behave or be in this way- empathetic, open, honest, less or non-judgmental toward others, and generous with help. There is a desire to give without expecting or wishing to receive something in return. Cortisol, insulin, estrogen, progesterone, and testosterone will be more balanced and even, blood sugar is more regulated, the heartbeat even and slow, and blood pressure balanced. The body does not retain water, nor is the body over-dehydrated. These are the key characteristics that should be occurring when the emotional body is in perfect balance with itself.

The way to bring the emotional body into balance include, anything that releases emotion, tension, stress, and anxiety—this will create clear, running waters with fewer rocks or less damning of the stream. Depending on the person this might require something like meditation, dance cardio, a comedy club, or breathing techniques. Ultimately, the emotional body comes into great balance when we learn how important it is to balance our hormones. Yoga, especially restorative and hatha, sauna, light detoxing or fasting (with adrenal and liver support), more touch and intimacy are key. Forgiveness and acts of forgiveness are also crucial. Learning the value of emotional intelligence and not only mental intelligence is central to empathetic and adrenal wellness and allowing the state of the emotional body to be in great harmony with itself and it's many different areas.

The Mental Body

The mental body is the third major part of the body that makes up the common processes that make us as a whole, and the parts that represent this part of the body include: our thoughts, attitudes, judgments, and prejudices—also how we perceive our worth and value in the world. Some people feel the mental body is actually a foot or several inches out in diameter from our physical selves.

The mental body represents all things intellectual, including analytical thought, how we process information, how we learn in school, and how we use our words. It also includes focus, clarity, direction, and contributions to creation and society. It is a key element in our thoughts becoming reality.

There are ways to bring the mental body into balance and this includes: Kundalini yoga, moderate cardio, talk therapy with an emotionally intelligent leader, and being in touch with emotions and spirituality for balance. The type of person living mostly in the mental body tends to overthink and doesn't let go of emotional strife or forgive easily or often. They might need to work through old emotional issues from the beginning of their life, and often need a mental release, which most frequently comes from strong emotional support or through a mentor who can lead them through positive stress releasing actions, and other ways of increasing their levels of positivity.

The Spiritual Body

The spiritual body is the fourth part of the body that makes up all parts of us as living beings and this consists of connection to all things, including the earth/self, to what we call God, the universe, the beyond, the divine, or higher self. This provides protection, union, help, and guidance from an outside source as well as from those who have passed on. It connects us to all that is. This is the element that no one and no situation stands alone, that we are all connected, and that it always takes more than one body to create all that exists in life. This is the brightest and the outermost area or ring in our aura or energetic field. The spiritual body is the most important part of our spiritual area and spiritual growth and has the most value when it comes to our immortal and spirit self. It allows us to see within our own being, our chakras, and the divine us that exists within.

The spiritual body is mostly feminine and is the unity of all living things, including the union between our soul, life experience, and destiny. This is not about going to church. In fact, it has little to do with religion.

The spiritual body is generally calm, fearless, highly creative, and operating without limits—paired with the fortitude and support to create action from ideas, when it is balanced and in perfect harmony with the rest of the body and with itself. Along with this comes the notion that there's a higher force guiding and protecting the project, and that there is something bigger at play than the normal human self. The spiritual body represents the synthesis and balance of the other three—it is the idea that we are greater than the sum of our parts.

Ways of bringing the spiritual self into balance include meditation, breathwork, gratitude, humbleness, generosity, and the act of giving, and acting accordingly. Also, it is very important to connect personal gain with universal oneness, and to understand that heaven is within a person's own self, that you are always in caring company, and no one physically holds your key to ultimate, consistent joy, except you. There is also the means of meditation, balancing your chakras, cleansing your internal self and your soul body. These are also ways you can bring your spiritual self in complete harmony and balance. It's important to constantly cleanse the internal self in order to bring yourself to a higher state of complete balance and harmony within.

Chapter 2

SPIRITUALITY UNDERSTOOD

Spirituality is a beautiful facet of life that brings a unique depth to each and everything you experience or undergo, and it helps to assist with other facilities as well. Spirituality can take many forms from religious beliefs and practices to the search for inner peace. It involves connecting to something bigger than oneself, understanding one's place in the world, and gaining insight into life's meaning and purpose. Spirituality can be seen as a journey of self-discovery and personal growth that helps individuals find greater clarity, balance, and contentment in life. By exploring spiritual topics such as faith, hope, love goodness and joy, we can come to better understanding ourselves while also deepening our appreciation of others around us.

Spirituality is an individual's own exploration of their relationship with the universe and its mysteries. It often involves trying to find meaning, purpose, or connection in life through rituals, meditation, self-reflection, and contemplation. By engaging with spiritual practices such as prayer, chanting mantras or studying sacred scriptures we can gain greater insight into our lives. Spirituality can help us learn how to respond more lovingly to ourselves and others while also allowing us to build a stronger sense of connection with something bigger than ourselves. Ultimately it helps us cultivate a deeper understanding of who we are and what matters most in life.

Spirituality is the manner and method by which we live our daily lives through the lens of compassion, higher awareness, and through our wonderful, amazing souls which are the purest part of our selves and the parts of us that are full of love and light, as opposed to the human part of us which exists usually through primitive or animalistic means. The soul is the gateway to love, light, joy, harmony and bliss and we should live through the means of our soul as the way of grasping the spiritual concepts of love and of life itself.

Spirituality radiates the beauty that is you within and allows you to be the better part of yourself as opposed to the parts of you that are your human and material self. Spirituality allows you to be a better you and a greater you and allows you to develop parts of your spiritual body including your chakras, your auras, your higher self, and your inner soul being. It allows those parts to develop through you, take over you and allows you to radiate your soul being and aura and be a better you and someone who loves being spiritual, holy, and who is at greater peace within yourself.

Spirituality is the beauty that is within us all, and the love within that humbles us all into decreasing or eliminating all arrogance and hatred that may be present within us, and letting us live a life of beauty, ease, and light full of only heavenly goodness mixed with that which allows us to be the best people we can be, minus any form of evil, hatred or prejudice within ourselves.

We understand, spirituality as a concept, that we know not a whole lot of though it is something that we understand we're capable of learning more of since spirituality is a huge part of our lives, and a huge part of our understanding and living deep within.

Spirituality is a part of our central lives, that we don't fully understand or have grasped, and much about yet we need to come to the greater understanding that this part of ourselves is a very important aspect of our ways of life and living and something we need to understand and come to greater terms with. We are spiritual beings deep within ourselves and we need to develop those parts of ourselves to be a greater part of our souls and higher selves.

Spiritual natures within us are the key to holding and grasping the very natures of our souls within and elevating that which is a part of our whole entity and transforming us into the love and light that we hold within ourselves. We believe ourselves to be whole and unique and we are, but somewhere we are also a greater part of the spiritual masses of people out there, thrilled to be part of something far greater than our own unique selves.

The concept of spirituality is about the belief in the unseen and something that is a greater part of our material human selves. People who follow religion can be spiritual people, and people who are spiritual are able to follow religion as well. Religion doesn't always play into the concept of spirituality though in most cases as stated people who are religious do follow many spiritual ideations and ways of life and belief systems. Religion is an organized set of beliefs or a belief system, whereas spirituality is a belief system or a way of achieving a different state of consciousness and way of living or a belief system in the spiritual part of a person or seeking a higher understanding of that which is spiritual in nature.

Spirituality transcends and describes a set of beliefs and experiences that a person may have, and it leans towards a way of life and practice of that which isn't material but that which is spiritual in nature. Spirituality focuses more on personal and life experiences, as opposed to religion which is more doctrine based and often structured. It can include a belief in a higher power, a search for something more than the material or physical, a belief in the soul and soul processes, and a varied or different way of life other than the normal life that most humans are used to being a part of or living in. The spiritual life is one which relies on being a part of spirit or nature as opposed to living in a technologized society, and relying on what most people do these days. People living the spiritual life tend to focus on pondering upon life's journeys, attempting to seek the answers to life and this world, philosophical quests and discoveries, and the appreciation of nature, love, life, and the world itself.

The appreciation for the gift of life

Once a person embarks on a spiritual journey, they will gain a greater appreciation for everything that is love, life and nature and understand that life itself is a beautiful blessing and gift that we must all live for happily and appreciate rather than look down upon. Also, a person embarking on a spiritual quest learns that there is not much substance to life or this world, except the beauty that is life and that there is more to living on this planet including the helping or aiding of those who are down or suffering or the helping of others. Once you've reached any form of awareness, you learn these lessons very fast.

You also learn the many blessings of this life, and that there is so much more to life than we ever give credit for. We were blessed with and given this amazing gift of living, and it should be embraced each and every moment no matter what. And that we should embrace the gift of life with every breath we take, and thank our Creator for this beautiful, amazing blessing given to us. We must cherish each and every waking moment we possess on this planet with the gift of life, love, and the utmost gratitude towards our Creator, and love and appreciate anything that is nature or natural for that is which is truly pure on this planet- the goodness of nature and the many blessings associated with it.

It is with the most gratitude, love, and joy that we accept the many blessings given to us on this planet. Many people tend to stray from this belief and concept and live in a state of negativity and disharmony. They tend to get caught up in their daily lives and often forget the concept of beauty and goodness that is present in our everyday worlds and daily lives. They feel as if life is too difficult to deal with, their problems are too much to be able to handle and they often just get caught up in the issues of this world and their own lives and turn to becoming very negative or pessimistic. It is with extreme gratitude that we must live, and the love for the blessings of this life and the gift that it has been that is bestowed upon us. Without the gift of life, we wouldn't exist, and wouldn't be able to count the many blessings we do cherish and hold, and we wouldn't be able to live our daily life the way we can.

Spirituality is the greater appreciation for the gift of life. We must learn to live each day with love, gratitude especially, extreme beauty and joy. We must understand the importance of appreciating each and every moment of our life and learn to live in the very moments we exist in with glory, happiness and appreciation for everything that has been granted to us by our Creator. We didn't just come onto this planet on our own- we do have a Creator and God that gave us life on this planet and created us from the start. We must understand that the core concept of spirituality is accepting, loving, and appreciating everything that we are blessed with and loving the gift of life that has been bestowed upon us.

We understand spirituality as a concept, that we know not a whole of though, it is something we understand and we're capable of learning more of since it is a huge part of our lives, and a huge of our understanding and living deep within

Spirituality is a part of our cellular lives that we don't fully understand or have grasped so much about, yet we need to come to the greater understanding that this part of ourselves needs to be fully immersed within our soul beings and consciousness and let out so that we can further examine and allow things to grow.

Chapter 3

How To Raise Your Consciousness

What is the concept of consciousness and how does it relate to the belief and nature of spirituality? The consciousness is the higher awareness we possess deep within our great minds. Consciousness is the awareness of internal and external existence. We hold varying forms of consciousness within and every person has a different set of levels when it comes to their own perceptions and ideas regarding a person's conscious mind.

A person's consciousness can also involve becoming more aware of the spiritual qualities that we hold and possess within our own minds, bodies and souls. We are spiritual beings within our regular bodies, and once we grow in consciousness, we do so as well in spirituality and the awareness of our own selves and minds. There are varying levels of consciousness that a person can attain and understand. Some aspects of spiritual consciousness are love, goodness, no fear, joy, peace, and unity.

There are many ways to increase or raise your consciousness and your awareness in life and in spiritual aspects. We need to focus on the good that we can possess in our own lives, and the different elements of consciousness itself, and evolve from there and create the foundation to build upon those very core beliefs and foundations. There are several ways of increasing or raising your levels of consciousness and your awareness within your own life. Some of these aspects include: raising your vibration, focus on love and light, build upon positivity, eliminate fear in your life, remove all negativity in your life, increase your peace and harmony within your world. These are very important key methods when it comes to raising your consciousness and allowing yourself to become immersed in goodness, and love and light overall.

Raise your vibration

Raising your vibration is a very important and key method in raising your levels of consciousness and awareness. It's extremely important that you don't live in the phases of being in darkness, away from the light, or living in modes of fear, negativity, hatred, darkness, or any of the lower vibrational forces. The reason for this is, any of these lower vibrational forces or beliefs, will not only bring you down, but it will bring disharmony into your life, create disease in your body, further spread negativity within your world and life, and rarely to never allow you to progress or succeed. These negative factors hinder all forms of goodness and progression and people become stuck in cycles of negativity. You'll want to stray away from all negative thoughtforms and focus on being incredibly good positive people and only go towards raising your vibration in a major way.

Ways to raise your vibration include: eating healthy higher-vibration foods that resonate with your energy levels, taking up sunshine and positive beneficial activities, repeating positive mantras to yourself, having positive beneficial beautiful thoughts as opposed to fear-based negative ones, thinking in a positive way all the time, leaving all fear-based thoughts and beliefs and straying towards positive ones, meditation and prayer, fasting, increasing your compassion, and doing anything that is good or full of love and light rather than of the darkness.

There are many other ways of raising your vibration including getting enough sleep, getting enough exercise, journaling positive thoughts, writing down your goals and undertaking them successfully, repeating positive affirmations towards yourself, hanging out with other high vibration people, and talking to your higher self. These are all ways you're able to raise your vibration and your semblance of spiritual and divine consciousness and allow yourself to transform into a powerhouse of divine consciousness, positivity, goodness, and bring forth your spiritual gifts and raise your spiritual awareness in a huge and amazing way in order to further benefit your life and allow you to evolve and grow into a greater spiritual being and person that you were always meant to be.

Focus on love and light

It is of utmost importance that you as a spiritual being and human trying to grow in consciousness and harmony focus on the ultimate which is love and light. What is the importance of love and light? Well divine love is the core and key attribute of being a highly spiritual person and one of the key ways of becoming an enlightened person and is a by-product itself of enlightenment. Once you become enlightened you are engulfed in love and light and this is what you eventually are or become, and it is of extreme importance that you focus on these key elements if you want to grow as a spiritual being.

If you want to raise your spiritual consciousness, you'll want to become that which is love and true and pure love only. True and pure love is a light and bliss energy that is of holy and true beauty and love, and it is the love that comes directly from God and the higher realms and dimensions that we usually don't have access to. When you raise your consciousness, you begin to access the higher dimensions and only then are you able to access this love and light that is of the higher realms. Once you raise your consciousness and awareness, you're fully able to do this on a regular basis and it's a very easy thing to accomplish.

Build upon positivity:

One of the key elements to being an extremely spiritual person and raising your consciousness is to build upon positivity and being a positive well-rounded person full of goodness and all the elements of good and love that will allow you to become more spiritual overall. It is important to be an overall positive, happy, spiritual person and you'll need to build upon the positivity and goodness that you do possess and make sure you're focusing on that which is harmony, and joy only and cultivating those aspects of good and magnificence.

It's not always easy to build on the positive aspects of yourself, that which you are deep within, and that which you can cultivate inside of yourself, in order to grow into being the wonderful, happy, spiritual precious treasure that you are. We must cultivate good energy, good thoughts, and good karma and hone in on it and allow it to exponentiate so that we can become beacons of goodness and light energy, but far more so we can become these very beacons of goodness within ourselves and grow and gather into light and soul energy and radiate positivity and goodness throughout our entire selves.

Eliminate fear in your life

Another way to raise consciousness is to eliminate fear in your life and focus on love-based ideals and ways of living, thinking, and existing rather than any fear-based notions or ideations. It's very important to not live in a state of anything that is of the lower vibrations which include fear-based ideas, thoughts, beliefs, actions. These include anxiety, anger, hate, lust, greed, selfishness, darkness, dark thoughts, or any of the included concepts or feelings. We must focus on that which is love, light and harmony only and stray away from any concept of darkness, or fear-based ideations.

Focusing on fear and fearing to do things in life, or possessing the notion of fear can have many varying problems in a person's life. It can cause a person to be unable to handle everyday tasks and to live in a state of disharmony and even disease many times. Eliminating fear in your life is of the utmost importance, and it's extremely essential in order to cultivate a healthy state of mind and a positive outlook on life and everything that's a part of it.

Increase peace and harmony in your world

It's essential that you increase peace and harmony in your world, for it is of utmost importance that you thrive on this peace, harmony, love, light and bliss that you've found or discovered as opposed to being in the dark and living in a fear-based state of despair or darkness.

Peace is an incredibly important aspect to have in your life in order to gain greater spiritual strength and a higher vibration. In order to raise your consciousness, you will need to gain greater peace in your life and reality and the way of doing this is through meditation, breathing exercises, quiet contemplation, and gaining a general awareness of everything in your presence.

There are a number of ways you can increase peace in your life. Contemplating in nature is another way you can gain a greater sense of peace, harmony and appreciation for all that is natural and good, and for the greater goodness of that which was created by the Creator. Nature is one of the best ways to gain a better sense of peace and goodness and it's one of the most effective ways of gaining a better connection with yourself and developing your inner self through.

Nature is one of the most important and effective ways of gaining the highest sense of peace and good, and gaining a harmony within yourself and with your surroundings.

By elevating the peace in your life, you can raise your consciousness levels in a major way and come to a better understanding and better terms with your state of mind and way of thinking. Your vibration increases and you can gain a much higher state of mind and elevated thoughtforms once you achieve a certain level of spirituality and peace within yourself.

The consciousness is the part of our body and soul that is the self or the part of our mind that merges with the soul and turns into the moral center of ourselves and is the part of us that is about being one with awareness of our own selves, and of internal and external existence. The conscience is a completely different aspect and is more about the moral goodness of one's own conduct, intentions, or character together with a feeling of obligation to do right or be good. Consciousness is the individual awareness of your unique thoughts, memories, feelings, sensations, and environments.

Essentially, your consciousness is the awareness of yourself and the world around you. Raising your consciousness means that you become more open to reality as a whole and gain a greater awareness of all that is surrounding you or around you. It also is exploring and broadening your own perceptions of reality, reconnecting with others and nature, and learning how to control your own destiny by your actions and thoughts. Raising your level of awareness and perception allows you to better connect with yourself, others, your higher self, and allows you to gain a greater conscious understanding of everything that exists in your world and reality.

Other ways you can raise your levels of conscious thinking are by embracing nature, being healthy, meditating, learning gratitude, releasing your creative side, enjoying your own company, opening your chakras, letting go of fear, and listening to your inner voice.

Chapter 4

Spiritual Awakening

What is spiritual awakening?

What is spiritual awakening and why is it so important in the scheme of things when it comes to spirituality?

A spiritual awakening is a great shift in consciousness or awareness where an individual experiences a deep connection to their inner self, a higher power or to the universe. It can involve a sense of purpose and a major transformation in one's beliefs and perspectives and allows a person to grow towards being a more spiritual person and allows a person to develop spiritually into higher levels.

The signs of a spiritual awakening can include a heightened intuition, increased empathy, a larger desire for personal growth, and a sense of being connected with all living beings. A spiritual awakening is your spiritual self growing and awakening and becoming more aware of what spirituality is, and with awakening there can come many different symptoms. You are in fact stretching yourself from your ego and awakening to a shift in perspective and to a different form of awareness- a spiritual one.

A spiritual awakening can take place immediately, over a short period of time, or it can take place gradually over long periods of time and occur for even decades and represent many different elements of spirituality within a person as the time goes by and all the symptoms have come through.

Sometimes, when a person is undergoing spiritual awakening, they have many different symptoms that can be almost painful or exhausting and when this happens, a person is undergoing something called 'spiritual crisis' and they are in need of a spiritual healer or counselor who can help guide them through their awakening. Sometimes energetic changes take place within a person or there is a fluctuation in energy, mood, diet, and other occurrences that do take place that can cause great alarm for a person, and they are in need of a spiritual therapist who can help guide them through if they are lucky enough to be able to find one.

A spiritual awakening can be one full of bliss and ecstasy while undergoing an opening of the spiritual senses which include the energy chakras, energetic points in the body, kundalini energy, and other important aspects within a person spiritually. However, spiritual awakening can also be a very tumultuous experience that isn't always roses and fairies and bliss energy and can encompass a host of other spiritual or otherworldly experiences which can involve anything from twin flames, to past life traumas manifesting in this reality, and scenarios occurring at exponentiated rates and very fast patterns.

This happens because when a person is awakening spiritually, many spiritual processes from other lifetimes, past lives and other worlds take place at a rapid pace, or even a slow pace, and will come forth, sometimes like a roller coaster effect and there is not much a person can do to stop this except study learn and understand the root cause behind what is occurring so they can best handle the situation at hand and grow from this experience.

Many spiritual experiences turn into mini lessons and means for us to grow as people, allow soul growth and grow spiritually in nature in order to better ourselves and take our souls to the next levels in this world and in the next. We are not just physical beings here on this planet once or twice- many of us have lived many lifetimes, in other worlds and have hundreds or thousands of past lives, and much of what is manifesting in this current reality that we are experiencing is happening as a result of what happened in past lives.

Sometimes, when we awaken spiritually, many spiritual elements of past lives come into play and sometimes they will begin to happen at a rapid pace. The same people you are dealing with in this world in fact you may have dealt with in a previous or other life in a similar scenario and it's important to understand the roles that people in this lifetime and in your world play now, compared to the roles they may have played in other lifetimes. This will help you better understand what is happening during your spiritual awakening.

Many times, when a person is undergoing a spiritual awakening, they are full of a plethora of energy that has a plethora of creations within the energy. This can be other beings, traumas, and spiritual junk or garbage that has latched onto the awakening. There are other beings which tend to attach to an awakening and will steal the energy of the person that is being harnessed. With the spiritual awakening, there is going to be a large amount of spiritual energy that is present within a person around a person and just everywhere surrounding and within that person.

If a person does not have the faculties and knowledge to know how to protect themselves, and to know how to channel this energy, and to store it somewhere else, then there will be a host, or various creatures that could latch onto a person and actually feed off the energy that is being cultivated and developed by the spiritually awakening person.

There are many key symptoms that people may encounter when they awaken spiritually. These can include

Feeling detached and anxious about what is happening

In the beginning of awakening, the spiritual process can feel overwhelming and difficult and sometimes people get anxious and confused about the entire process and are in dire need of guidance or support from a spiritual therapist or someone who knows what a spiritual awakening entails.

Reevaluating your beliefs

Spiritual awakening can cause you to reevaluate many of your belief and the system you grew up thinking. How you perceive life, your religious beliefs, and many things that you grew up believing or thinking may seem different than before. You will change how you prioritize your beliefs and the manner in which you perceive your life and spirituality in general

Spiritual concepts become more important

As spirituality makes its way into your life through an awakening or by other means, the idea and concept of spirituality becomes extremely important to you and you find yourself researching and learning more about the process. This is a calling for you and it becomes a huge part of your life now as opposed to the past when you didn't think much about it.

You will find many spiritual concepts just appearing into your life causing you to do mass amounts of research to further attempt to understand what exactly is happening in your life.

You will want to become a spiritual teacher

Most people who undergo a spiritual awakening have the great desire to be a spiritual teacher, leader or feel a strong desire to teach others about the important lessons they have learned. Most people who have undergone an awakening have a strong calling and desire to teach or be a spiritual healer, leader or a guru to the masses. They will want to use their newfound knowledge to teach and heal the masses and tell everyone about what spirituality is and the many lessons there are to know.

Your dreams become vivid and life-like

For many, their dreams may become vivid or more life-like once they awaken spiritually. They will discover that their dream world and life might even be better than their regular humanly life and may even begin to control their dreams, which is the concept of lucid dreaming and take it even further. People soon learn the importance of dreams and sometimes your dreams might even be able to foretell your future.

Your psychic abilities develop

For many, one's psychic abilities begin to develop at a rapid pace, and once you awakening spiritually, you soon learn that you have a host of psychic abilities that are ready accessible to you so you can help and heal others and help others in their journey as well. Abilities you never knew that even existed within you will soon appear to you and you will learn that you have greater abilities than you knew of.

You can use your abilities to help others grow and become better people and use them to help yourself as well in your own spiritual journey.

Spiritual aspects occur at a rapid pace

You'll soon find yourself encountering a large host of encounters with all sorts of spiritual concepts such as synchronicities, which are instances or experiences that happen based on specific phenomena in your life. Concepts within spirituality will begin to happen- you will soon meet your soulmates, twin flames, and many other people will come into your life in a very spiritual manner such as people from past lives.

Very special and specific occurrences will happen which are highly spiritual in nature and you may be bombarded with experiences from other lifetimes that begin to manifest in this one such as past life traumas, recurrent events from past lives which are still taking place in this lifetime with the same people, and even experiencing special numerology such as angelic numbers repeating themselves to attempt to show you the importance and specificity of what is occurring in your current lifetime.

It's important to learn and understand what this all means so you can grow from it. Sometimes phenomenon can occur at a rapid and confusing pace so it's important to seek guidance from a certified spiritual therapist or counselor who can help you understand exactly what is happening so you can learn from these lessons, grow and help others as well.

You feel an abundance of love and bliss

One sign of spiritual awakening is the feeling of extreme bliss energy and light and love and this is a sign that a person is undergoing a spiritual awakening. You end up being bombarded with a large amount of beautiful love and light energy and feel a love for every living creation and feel a strong connection with others.

Your empathy becomes heightened

When you awaken spiritually, your empathy and compassion become very heightened. You find yourself feeling a strong love and desire to help others and you have a strong care for other people's feelings and for all creatures in general. Your empathy will become more heightened once you are going through an awakening.

You may find yourself isolated for some reason

Many times, when a person is going through an awakening, they find themselves isolated since many people don't understand what they are going through, and might even put a person down for feeling the strong feelings and experiences they are having or even shun them in a sense. A lot of times, a person undergoing an awakening is purposely put through this form of isolation so they can learn how to become true masters and master the art of becoming true gurus and understanding the concept of awakening and enlightenment and the purpose of isolation.

You want to help others

You will find yourself wanting to be of service to others, and you feel a greater connection with others and wanting to help and be very selfless. You learn the concepts of grace and patience more, and want to serve others endlessly, humans, animals or even the environment. You soon learn that this is the most important lesson and aspect in life- to be on this planet to help others and that is the true purpose and reason why we are here.

Nature becomes very important to you

Nature becomes a very important element to you and you will feel a greater connection to nature and to the natural elements such as plants, animals and the environment. You will feel a respect and admiration for nature as opposed to how you may have felt before and will notice the importance of it and its presence in the planet.

Your senses become more heightened

For many people their senses become more heightened, and they become more aware of their lives, their surroundings, and their overall awareness increases drastically. They become more aware of the concept of being in the present moment or living in the moment and other spiritual notions and ideations.

Your awareness increases

Your general awareness increases and you become more aware of scenarios and situations that occur in your life. You become more aware of each and every little thing that occurs in your life, and what goes on in your thoughts. Overall, you become a more aware person of everything that happens in your life and become more observant and keen about certain things.

Physical symptoms such as fatigue and brain fogging

Some people experience many physical symptoms of spiritual awakening such as fatigue or even brain fogging. Some people experience elevated moods and may cry a lot or laugh or might experience a host of varying physical issues as a result of this awakening. If a person is experiencing physical symptoms it's very important that they seek help from a spiritual therapist or spiritual crisis counselor who can help them with their current situation.

Chapter 5

THE SPIRITUAL ELEMENTS

What are the spiritual elements?

What are the spiritual elements one might ask? The spiritual elements are the various types of aspects within spirituality whether it be events, occurrences or phenomena which are spiritual in nature and can be defined by the concepts within spirituality. This chapter will list many various elements in spirituality and give the definitions and their importance within the spiritual world.

The spiritual elements are extremely important for they make up the spiritual world and the ideas within spirituality itself. Many people aren't familiar with these concepts or terms so this will give you some insight into exactly what these elements are and what they mean and how they might play into your life spiritually or in some other format.

These spiritual elements tend to increase or become more prominent when a person is undergoing a spiritual awakening and people will notice these phenomena to become more prevalent and occur at a far more rapid pace. People will also notice these elements to come into play once they begin to spiritually awaken and will notice these situations come into existence and will become introduced to these things naturally when this awakening takes place.

Past life friend or soulmate

There are people that will come into your life who might be predominant in your life, however, what you'll find is that many of these people actually existed in your past life in one or many forms and are now in your life in this world as well, sometimes and often playing the same roles they played during your experience with them in other lifetimes or worlds.

You will find that in your current life, you will find that many people such as immediate family members or close friends held places in your world in other lifetimes and held significance in your life in some form and are now replaying a similar pattern in this life and world that they did in other lifetimes.

Synchronicities

Synchronicities are recurring signs or patterns that are perceived by someone or that do occur that are coincidences with regards to something in a person's life. They can occur spiritually in many different forms, and they usually are a sign that there is a message that is being given to a person through them or that a person is on a particular path.

Spiritual synchronicities are orchestrated and aligned in a very strategic manner to deliver a message, give guidance or give us reassurance that we're on the right path.

Once we awaken spiritually, synchronicities become very apparent and can occur at a rapid pace simply because there are many spiritual messages being given to a person and this is one way it is done. We become mirrors spiritually and as a result whatever we are projecting will come back to us or manifest in our lives in some form. Synchronicities will often occur at a very rapid pace and people will begin to notice strange coincidences happen that are very uncanny and when you witness a pattern of coincidences you are dealing with synchronicities.

Carl Jung defined synchronicity in psychological terms as "a meaningful coincidence of two or more events where something other than the probability of chance is involved." He believed it occurred when our brains make connections across space and time. He used the term to describe circumstances that appear meaningfully related yet lack a causal connection. Jung developed the theory of synchronicity as a noncausal principle serving as the objective connection between these seemingly meaningful coincidences. The event is meaningful because what happens in the external world is mirroring something that is happening in one's internal world.

Within spirituality, spirit or any of your guides will send synchronicities as helpful information regarding your destiny, and as ways for healing and personal growth. Sometimes they can come from our own soul or intuition or a part of our higher selves. They happen when our spiritual selves want to send us information or a message to help guide us in some form.

If you witness the numbers 555, 222 or patterns of numbers, this can occur as a numerological synchronicity that occurs within the means of spiritual significance. There are many links to specific numbers and their significance within these patterns.

If you're going through old pictures and suddenly witness an old friend, and days later that friend just happens to show up in your life somehow or gives you a call, you just experienced a synchronicity that is there to assist you in some form when it comes to this particular person being a part of your life, or something of a similar significance.

Synchronicities can occur in the form of numbers, through music messages, repetitions, people, colors, animals, sounds, nature, symbols, words of others, dreams and unexplainable phenomena.

Generally, if a person is undergoing a spiritual awakening, they will experience a plethora of synchronicities, signs, and many meaningful phenomena with regards to spiritual aspects in this manner. They will deal with a number of synchronicities happening on a grand scale and level that will not only happen back to back but will occur for a long or extended period of time.

Parallels

Parallels are similar to synchronicities except they occur as parallels to other events that occurred such as the repeating or mirroring of an event or circumstance that has happened repeatedly. Parallels don't appear similar to coincidences or déjà vu, the way synchronicities or events that continue occurring are. They are in fact the exact same event or occurrence just repeating itself in a similar pattern or manner, and happening in a very similar manner as an event or experience that has already happened in a person's life.

For example, if Cynthia had things happening in her life that occurred over and over again, and she kept seeing the same signs then that would be considered a synchronicity. A parallel would be if the same event kept happening and mirroring itself then it would be considered a parallel and something that just keeps happening and is a mirror for itself in a sense.

Twin flames

Twin flames are believed to be two halves of the same soul, yet they are not considered to be soulmates. They often mirror each other and will tend to have a pattern of similar lives and similar patterns of events occurring throughout their lifetime. Some signs of a twin flame are a sense that you're meeting yourself, uncanny and multiple similarities, a deep connection, a desire to grow, the meeting signifies a great change in your life.

Twin flames will feel extremely connected on a very spiritual and personal level and their lives may mirror one another's. You will notice many similarities going on between the two of you and it will almost seem like the other person is your twin or very similar to yourself. Twin flames are seen as a soul that has been split in two, while the concept of soulmates are two separate souls coming together for a divine or other purpose.

Twin flame relationships can be very tumultuous and bring forth a great amount of chaos and upheaval to someone's life, whereas a soulmate relationship is the complete opposite- it brings support and soulmates often complement one another. There are actually various stages of a twin flame relationship that have been categorized and described. These stages are yearning, meeting, the honeymoon phase, and challenges emerge, the test, the chase and surrender. They also often come into your life and expose all the issues that you have been going through in life. Many narcissistic relationships are mislabeled and may actually be twin flame relationships.

Soulmates

Soulmates are often kindred souls and spirits that will come together in some form of harmony. People who are soulmates often feel they are linked at the soul level in some form and often times in a very extraordinary manner. There are varying types of soulmates out there including soul partners, soul ties, karmic soulmates, and companion soulmates. Each of these types of soulmates signifies some form of a soul connection. Not every soulmate has to be a romantic one, and there are platonic soulmates as well as companion ones as well.

Some people come together as soulmates for karmic reasons, and others come together even in large or family groups. Karmic relationships may come into our lives as agents who create opportunities to improve our karma through positive, negative or even neutral means. Large groups of souls can exist in soul families. This can exist as family members in this lifetime or even people who aren't family members who come together for a common cause.

There are also soul contracts which are agreements you make on a soul level to do certain or important things in this lifetime. Soul contracts can exist in many different means and for various aspects with regards to accomplishing specific tasks to contracts that exist in order to enhance spiritual growth.

Soul partners are the most common type of soulmate. You agreed to partner with specific souls in this lifetime in all kinds of formats- from best friends, to business partners. A soul partnership can be with someone you have known your whole life or even someone that you have known for a short period of time. They are designed to support you in this life in many different forms, from physical to emotional, and to assist you with accomplishing many different purposes you may have on this planet.

Spiritual Crisis

Spiritual crisis is a scenario or situation when a person has been through a significant spiritual change in their life and there are many different symptoms associated with this change, and the many various aspects having to do with a scenario regarding this type of situation. This is a form of crisis where an individual experiences major changes to their system within their life because of a spontaneous spiritual experience. A spiritual crisis can cause significant disruption in psychological, social and occupational functioning.

Spiritual experiences that are thought to lead to spiritual crisis or spiritual emergency are complications related to near-death experiences, kundalini syndrome, paranormal experiences, mystical experiences, existential crisis, and other spiritual practices.

Powerful feelings, inner experiences and physical sensations may come forth that are overwhelming and unfamiliar, and people may be in need of spiritual guidance in order to learn how to cope with this type of spiritual crisis or phenomena. When supported and with the right guidance, spiritual crisis can lead to deeper levels of awareness and connection to spirit and to our divine selves and to greater beneficial spiritual experiences.

Higher self

The higher self is the part of us that has transcended the ego, and it is the higher portion of our consciousness and exists in the higher and more divine realms. It is the part of us that is connected to the divine. Our higher self is truly our greatest potential. Our higher self knows our true purpose and helps us to live a more fulfilled and wonderful life full of joy and peace and spiritual growth and self-awareness.

The higher self can also be known as the inner self that is separate and distinct from our personality. It is the higher portion of our being and though it is a part of our soul, it exists and functions in a different format than the soul. It is there to help, assist, and guide us when we need its help with regards to many different aspects of our life.

Kundalini energy

Kundalini energy is a strong energy that is located down the base of the spine. It is known as the divine feminine energy, that is the shakti or goddess energy and sometimes known as serpent energy. Within Hindu belief, it is the creative power and energy of the universe. It is believed to lie dormant at the base of the spine and one of the reasons of Yoga practice is to awaken this energy.

Once awakened, kundalini energy travels up the spinal region through channels called nadis, activating each of the seven main chakras along the way. Awakened or activated kundalini energy can help a person reach enlightenment. Many people experience an awakening of kundalini energy and undergo spiritual awakening or even spiritual crisis because of the nature of this kind of energy.

Chapter 6

Six fundamental principles in spiritual practice

Spiritual practices encompass a wide range of activities and rituals that individuals engage in to cultivate a deeper connection with the sacred, the divine, or their inner selves. Some common spiritual practices include:

Meditation: Focusing the mind to achieve a sense of inner peace and clarity.

Prayer: Communicating with a higher power, expressing gratitude, or seeking guidance.

Yoga: Combining physical postures, breath control, and meditation for holistic well-being.

Mindfulness: Cultivating awareness of the present moment to reduce stress and enhance spiritual connection.

Rituals and Ceremonies: Participating in formalized actions to mark significant events or connect with the divine.

Fasting: Temporarily abstaining from food or certain activities for spiritual reflection and discipline.

Chanting and Affirmations: Using repetitive sounds or positive words to focus the mind and uplift the spirit.

Pilgrimage: Undertaking a journey to a sacred place for spiritual exploration or worship.

Study of Sacred Texts: Engaging with religious or philosophical texts for guidance and inspiration.

Acts of Compassion and Service: Practicing kindness and helping others as a way of expressing spiritual values.

These practices can be tailored to individual beliefs and preferences, serving as tools for personal growth, self-discovery, and connection with the spiritual realm.

There are six important fundamental and core principles that allow a person access to a greater spiritual path and to the path of love, light and true enlightenment, awakening and spiritual bliss. These six fundamentals are:

1. Belief in the creator
2. Belief in the beauty and purity of nature
3. Focus on the access to the higher self and soul
4. Seeking the path to goodness and purity
5. Seeking quietness of the mind
6. The path to spiritual awakening

These are the core and fundamentals to spiritual practice and spirituality and these basic principles will allow a person to become a more spiritually enlightened and fulfilled human being and one who is more in harmony with their own selves and with the Creator as well and with light energy, goodness, and bliss. These six fundamental principles allow a person to gain greater access to the spiritual world and let them cultivate the way to being greater spiritual beings and grow in spiritual strength.

These basics of spirituality are what can allow a person to become more spiritual and head towards the path of enlightenment and grow their inner ethereal vision and self, and become overall greater spiritual people and beings in the collective consciousness of the planet and the world we reside in.

Belief in the Creator

Belief in the creator is a key element within spiritual practice and is the core of spiritual belief. There are many people out there who don't believe in the concept of a Creator or a God. Many of these people feel as if there is no such thing as creationism and believe that humans and animals evolved throughout the history of time into the kinds of species and beings they are now. The only issue here is that even with evolution, there can still be the concept and idea of the Creator who originally created these creatures. Even if evolution does exist or is the basic truth, it doesn't refute the notion of there being a Creator.

There are many hard-core believers in the concept of there not being a Creator or someone who created humankind or this planet. One of the first aspects to the concept of spiritual practice is the acknowledgment of there being a Creator or a God who created this planet and all that is in it. The concept of belief in a God who created this planet is the very core and basis for all that is spiritual and all that exists for none of what we perceive or live through can ever exist without the concept of the Creator there.

The sole reason any or everything exists on this planet is linked directly to the concept of the Creator or the being who people call "God." Without God's creation none of us would exist, and nothing that which we love, experience, and use to better ourselves would exist either. All praise is given to the Creator for without the Creator, plants would not exist, nor would the concept of meditation. Life as we know it would not exist without God having created this very concept.

The number one key to spiritual practice and spiritual belief is the core of anything that we as living beings on this planet should believe in, and that is the concept, acknowledgment, and recognition of the gifts given to us by God the Creator of all things on this planet, and the concept that we have no clue of the truths of anything since we are limited and mortal creations of God. All praise is given to the Creator for without Him, we would not have nature and all that is beautiful on this planet to contemplate on, appreciate, and be a part of. We wouldn't exist as well and the key to being a spiritual person is the acknowledgment and recognition and praise of God the Creator.

The planet wasn't created by itself, and it definitely didn't come into existence due to a random "big bang" that simply happened to occur. Everything came into fruition and existence through the Creator God, and God the Creator has sent Prophets and humans to teach us the concept of who He is and how this planet which belongs to Him only was created and all the creatures that belong in it. Everything was created to perfection and we as spiritual beings need to validate this and appreciate the many blessings given to us by our Creator.

Belief in the beauty and purity of nature

The second basic principle to good spiritual practice and principles is the strict belief in the beauty of nature and a special belief that nature is a very unique and rare aspect of this planet that should be appreciated and is a key to being a happy and more spiritual person in general. Nature is a very important element in the concept of spirituality and spiritual beliefs. Nature can be a key source of spiritual inspiration for it evokes feelings of honor and inspiration in a person. Nature can sometimes be perceived as a manifestation of a higher power or a divine presence.

Nature is the physical world and everything that is comprised of it including animals, plants, landscapes, flowers, trees, leaves, and natural phenomenon. It encompasses the natural environment and world and the interactions between living beings and their surroundings.

Nature can actually enhance a person's spiritual experience by allowing a sense of tranquility, peace and a connection to something very natural and amazing. Many people are able to practice their spirituality through nature, and even within being a part of nature and their spiritual practices can be greatly enhanced by nature in various forms. Nature can also offer a place for spiritual reflection, meditation, and great contemplation, and allow people to feel more connected to other individuals and to the world around them and to tap into a deeper form of spirituality.

Nature's beauty and wonder can be a reminder of the great aspects it has to offer within the ideation of spirituality and how important it is within spirituality. It's important to respect and admire the wonder and greatness that nature, the plants, trees, leaves, and animals all are and how important their roles in spirituality are. Nature is an amazing, beautiful, wonderful and pure source of true and pure spirituality and we can not only learn from it but can become greater spiritual beings in the presence of it and can learn to be more spiritual in nature and use nature to practice our spiritual within.

Nature is one of the most important and key aspects to leading a more spiritual and beautiful life and is one of the key factors that can assist someone in becoming a more spiritual person. Appreciate nature for what it is and you are on your way to going into the gateway of true spirituality and love, for nature is the gateway to true love and spirituality. Nature is the purest of God's creations and should be respected, admired, acknowledged, and appreciated for it will allow you to grow spiritually within and become a better person overall and connect you to your higher self, to spirituality and to God.

Focus on the access to the higher self and to the soul

It is extremely important that we as living beings, humans and spiritual beings focus on the greater aspect of the higher self and on the soul. This is another key element to spiritual principles and practices. The higher self is a very important element of our own self and our soul. What is the higher self? the higher self can sometimes be considered the true self or the soul, or just a different, greater portion of ourself that is located in the higher dimensions and realms and which harnesses a greater aspect of ourselves and has is the key to all the answers about us and that which harbors extremely important secret and hidden knowledge which our human, material and conscious self has little access or understanding to.

Our higher self is a concept in spirituality and psychology that refers to the aspect of our being that is connected to our higher consciousness, wisdom and a greater purpose and understanding. It is perceived as the authentic and divine part of ourselves that transcends the ego and has a deeper and better understanding of our true nature, potential, past lives etc.

It is of great importance that we focus on the higher self when it comes to asking questions and being one with ourselves. The higher self has all the answers to anything we need to know and has knowledge of every lifetime we have lived and everything our soul has ever experienced and once we connect to our higher and divine self, we can gain the answers we need in our spiritual and even our worldly lives. In order to truly be spiritual people and those who are connected to our soul, the divine and to our spiritual selves, we need to learn how to access and talk to our higher self and to learn the important secrets it holds and harbors and to gain a greater understanding of our higher and divine self. Our higher self is far more important than our material physical and worldly self and is the essence of our soul and being and the understanding and acknowledgment of it is extremely important.

Gaining access to your higher self can involve meditation, self-reflection, and mindfulness. There are many health benefits one can achieve while connecting with their higher self. it can give you clarity, insight, a sense of inner peace, allow you to access your intuition, and let you understand your true purpose. You can also enhance your spiritual development and personal growth.

Seeking the path to goodness and purity

It is of extreme importance that as a spiritual person or someone who is awakening spiritually or gaining spiritual insight that a person is on the path to seeking overall goodness and purity. In order to be a more spiritual person, you must always be on the path to wanting more good and that which is beneficial into your life, rather than what is negative or something that might bring you down or not help with the overall collective good and harmony of the world.

One path to true spirituality is the one of great harmony and good and that is what you should always be seeking, yearning and wanting to achieve more of- to understand the concept of good and purity and wanting to be which is pure and good and not which is evil or harmful. Many people aren't always reflecting on what kind of people they are deep within, so they aren't always on this specific path, though it is of great importance to always be on this wavelength of thinking.

If we want to elevate our spiritual lives and even our worldly lives, then we must focus on being better people in general and do what we can to be better people and strive towards this goal in life. This is one of the few fundamental practices to becoming a more spiritual person and elevating our spiritual growth and taking ourselves to the next level and the many levels above that.

Seeking quietness of the mind

Without quietness of the mind, it's difficult to attain spiritual enlightenment, awakening or any form of nirvana. The mind for many people can usually be a place full of chaos, loudness, erratic thoughts, and many other qualities that people don't want their mind to be. Many people can sometimes struggle with this concept and can spend months to even decades attempting to quiet their mind so they can reach elevated levels of spiritual enlightenment, happiness, or various forms of bliss.

Quieting the mind is about calming the constant stream of thoughts, and distractions that occupy or take over our minds, and it leads to mental clarity, focus and greater peace. This also pertains to reducing chatter in the mind and achieving a sense of inner calm.

Quieting of the mind is a key concept when it comes to the idea of spirituality or spiritual enlightenment. You'll often learn about how meditation is a key means to quieting the mind and allowing a person to obtain some form of enlightenment or just reach elevated states of bliss energy and ecstasy by achieving this quietness of the mind. It is the blank slate of the mind which allows for a person to reach greater elevated levels and states of enlightenment and spirituality and is the foundation that people need to build upon when attempting to become more spiritually inclined people.

Meditation is one of the few great keys to quieting the mind and there are numerous health benefits to doing so as well. It can reduce stress and anxiety, improve focus and concentration, promote better sleep and help with overall mental well-being. Some techniques for quieting the mind are mindfulness, meditation, deep breathing exercises, muscle relaxation, journaling and spending good time in nature.

Mindfulness meditation is about focusing on the present moment in an elevated state of happiness. Deep breathing exercises help calm the nervous system, muscle relaxation is about tensing and relaxing various muscle groups, journaling can help release tension and organize thoughts, and spending time in nature can promote relaxation, eliminate stress and build on spiritual strength within a person.

The path to spiritual awakening

In order to become more spiritual people and become spiritually inclined, we must constantly seek the path to spiritual awakening. We can't just sit around and hope that we magically open spiritually and will transform into greater spiritual beings. We must be proactive in our inner search for spiritual enlightenment and awakening and this is a very important and key practice that will allow us to grow spiritually and become more awakened and spiritually open people.

We are spiritual beings deep within; however, we are living human and physical lives in this world. Many people get caught up in the bustle of being in this world, having to work jobs and do what they can to sustain themselves and their families. Although people might worship their God or follow religious beliefs, many people lack the time to focus on being spiritual people in general. In order to become spiritual and grow on a path, we must take the steps necessary in order to do this by focusing on spirituality and by doing techniques that will allow us to spiritually grow, transform, and awaken.

Spiritual awakening is a shift in consciousness where a person experiences a sense of connection to a higher power, the universe, or to their inner or higher self. It can involve a heightened awareness, sense of purpose in life and a greater bliss or inner peace.

During a spiritual awakening, people may experience a greater sense of compassion or empathy for living beings. They may feel a greater connectedness to all living creatures as well. This can lead to personal growth, amazing self-discovery, and a change in values and beliefs. A spiritual awakening is generally a personal journey that is brought on by exploring a person's beliefs, inner self, and morals.

The benefits of spiritual awakening can be grand and numerous and being on the path to spiritual awakening is a fundamental aspect in increasing your spiritual belief system and being on the path to spiritual mastery. This can include greater empathy for oneself and for others, enhanced self-awareness of a person's life and their surroundings, greater compassion, and a better sense of inner peace. A spiritual awakening can also lead to emotional healing, great personal growth, and a more fulfilling life.

A person can also become more intuitive, have improved mental and emotional well-being, and become more moral and spiritual people with better values overall. People can be happier and have gained a greater sense of joy and harmony as well. A spiritual awakening can lead to greater spiritual fulfillment and an overall better, happier life as a person can gain many different benefits from being a spiritually awakened person and can grow even further in their spiritual journey and take it to better and higher levels and become a spiritual master or guru eventually.

Personal growth can become tremendously impacted as well as people can become healed from an awakening. Emotional and physical healing are promoted, as well as the concept of introspection, and learning and gaining a higher awareness of a person and of others.

Chapter 7

You Can Achieve The Impossible

D o you feel as if you're just limited in what you're able to accomplish or undertake?

Does it feel as if you have limitations as a person because of the way you think?

It is possible to achieve the impossible

Do you feel, as if achieving the impossible as it is an extremely difficult feat to do? Do you believe that things in life are not as easy for you as they are for others? Do certain tasks just seem Impossible for you to accomplish? Well, look no further, because what you feel is impossible is actually extremely impossible to achieve and to do! The possible is there whether you believe it or not, and you are capable of achieving and accomplishing anything which you feel might be impossible.

It's important to believe in yourself and your dreams and goals in life and all of the different elements of this. We often tend to second guess ourselves and feel as if we're just not good enough to do many tasks we feel we need to accomplish in life.

Most people who find success in achieving the impossible didn't always believe in themselves or achieved these successes from a younger age so they were used to believing in their own selves and knew what their capabilities were from the start.

You'll find success stories everywhere from Venus Williams to Tom Brady and many of these highly success stories were not only able to achieve success, but to reach heightened levels of fame and fortune along with their success.

The impossible is there for you to reach. You just have to know exactly how to grasp and how to utilize it to your own benefit. You might think that it's extremely difficult to do tasks and hobbies and accomplish goals that just seem too far-fetched for you, but in reality, these goals are not too far-fetched for anyone, much less for yourself.

Well how do I know I can accomplish these goals?

How do you know you can actually accomplish these goals in your life? Well, there are many different means through which you know you're able to accomplish these goals. You are a capable human being, who is worthy of accomplishing just about any goal you'd like to accomplish in your life in the world and on this planet. You are not a limited, inferior, or lesser person such as you think of yourself often or how you tend to perceive yourself.

You actually possess no real limitations in the types and levels of capabilities you're able to achieve. The impossible is yours for you to achieve anytime you want, and with enough hard work, dedication and planning.

It's important to start off small and build from there gradually. Start planning your goals and activities or the event you want to accomplish or partake in and begin to start from there small steps, rather than starting off in a grand or large format and making huge mistakes or being unsure of what you're able to do.

Have you ever wanted to start a business yet just wasn't sure how to go about doing it? Start off gradually, take baby steps and first think of a good business idea, then slowly begin to think of ways you can implement this idea into something greater and turn it into something far more productive for yourself, rather than just a minor afterthought or a business ideation.

From there on, you'll want to grow your idea to something greater and bigger, and start off from there and go slow, take steps to create your idea, and figure out how you want to grow your business, market your business, and from there on, you can actually move forward into creating something that is amazing, productive and fantastic, as opposed to feeling as if you really weren't able to create a business for yourself, or do anything of that nature.

This is one of the few ways you can actually achieve the impossible to achieve the impossible something that is actually very possible and you can do it with a positive and successful state of mind and a state of mind that will allow you to turn your fears and confused emotions into success, positivity, something productive and a wonderful and grateful mindset. And eventually a successful business or asset that you can use for yourself into gaining monetary funds, creating a name or brand for yourself or creating something that is far more successful and achievable than what you currently have accomplished at this time.

Achieving the impossible is very real and you too can achieve this task if you only try and figure out what your strengths are and what you're truly capable of. You can learn what your true capabilities are from achieving the impossible or from accomplishing a plethora of goals and achievements, and you can definitely surprise yourself as well.

Is there a meter or way of gauging whether I'm able to do certain duties or important tasks in my life or world?

There is absolutely no meter or way of gauging what your abilities and capabilities are simply because you only learn what they are from actually accomplishing a specific task at hand. What you will learn is that your abilities are in fact, extremely unlimited rather than limited, and you are actually able to accomplish hundreds and thousands of things that you've previously had no idea that you were able to accomplish. This is why the impossible is very possible, and some that is definite for almost every person out there.

You will learn what your true capabilities are from experiencing and actually accomplishing these tasks and your specific goals, and once you do so then you'll begin to understand what your capabilities are, and how you can accomplish what you felt was once the impossible because now it is very possible. You will learn that you are limitless and are able to accomplish anything, for anything is possible with your capabilities.

I learned this concept through my own means as well, which is by accomplishing hobbies, tasks and goals which I felt were impossible for me to do or which seemed too difficult. The more I achieved, the more I learned that there was more and more I could do with my own hidden gifts and talents and that there was no real limit to what

I could accomplish, and that mine and every human's capabilities were limitless rather than being limited.

Spiritually, we can always achieve the impossible for higher self, as always, with us, guiding us and allowing us to lift up ourselves in our spirit and showing us that we are able to do anything that we want to do. We must allow our spiritual and higher selves to allow us to exist in the higher vibrations and allow those lessons to steer us in the direction of harmony and goodness, rather than any form of darkness or negativity.

Do away with self-doubt

We as people tend to be extremely self-critical self, doubtful, and feel as if it is extremely difficult for us to take on specific tasks or accomplish certain goals. This is not the case at all for we need to think, in terms of feeling, as if we are able and capable of pursuing and being successful at endeavors, rather than being critical of ourselves simply because being critical is not going to help the situation at all. We should never doubt our own abilities, our our own selves, and need to constantly think in terms of the fact that we are actually able to accomplish and do all the different things that we feel, or that we aren't able to do for this will allow us to actually accomplish these things, having a very positive and hopeful state of mind.

Not having a positive and hopeful state of mind will actually create in turn, all the negativity and the negative snowballing effects to occur. We actually create a negative situation for ourselves and create a snowballing effect for negativity to occur rather than for extreme positivity or good things to occur for the specific goal or task at hand to occur in a positive manner rather than a negative one.

Master the basics

Master the basics in your life. You must get adequate sleep, rest, nutrition, exercise, There are several ways you can utilize your goals and achieve the impossible. You must make sure that your needs are met in order to be able to achieve the impossible and achieve great and amazing feats. By being able to handle the basics, you're allowing yourself the means to better deal with the bigger and more major situations that you have to deal with.

Clear your calendar and create a brand new one

You have to learn to create boundaries, prioritize only the aspects that contribute to your goal, and not focus on anything except the goal at hand. This is only for the current time it's not for good. Once you clear your calendar of the busy, distracting stuff, make a game plan. Schedule daily tasks and weekly mini goals so you can reach new checkpoints each day.

This is one of the more effective ways of being able to accomplish the goal at hand and reach new achievements that seem impossible to do.

Work harder than you have worked before

Reaching goals and the impossible is not an easy task to do. It's not something that can be done in a minute or in a short period of time for it's going to take effort and means to achieve your desired dreams and what you feel might be of the impossible to achieve. You will have to face the hard work to get to the success.

Learn how to deal with failure

Success doesn't come easily and with the situation at hand, it's extremely important to learn to handle any form of failure for failure is a part of having to reach any form of success. Failure tends to happen very often so don't feel as if you are unable to achieve the goal in mind simply because you are dealing with failure or not getting things right immediately. Sometimes, it takes a long time and many strings of failure for a person to achieve any real form of success or to win at the given situation or to do what they set out to do. Nothing comes easy and that which you feel isn't possible surely doesn't come easily as well.

Take accountability for any mistakes you make or for your actions

It is important to take responsibility for any setbacks or any mistakes you make for in this case, you will allow yourself to be held responsible and then focus on making things better for yourself. If you miss an important meeting you had so that you can improve upon your project, you will need to make up for that meeting or reschedule it, rather than make excuses for your behavior, not take responsibility, or ignore the situation. If you do this then you'll often find yourself stuck in a bad situation or a rut, rather than moving forward. Allowing responsibility for the situation lets you acknowledge the facts of the situation, get a better grasp of what is going on and allows you to move ahead and further yourself and your goals rather than staying stuck in a stagnant situation where you feel nothing happened, and you did nothing wrong. It won't get you anywhere or be of any benefit to you to not take responsibility.

Stop making excuses

It's important to stop making excuses for yourself or for your actions because they will get you nowhere and will be of no real benefit to you. Excuses keep you trapped in your comfort zone and do not allow you to further yourself in your current goal or situation so it's important to leave them behind and get out of your comfort zone and focus on making those goals come true and happen.

When you hear that voice of excuse telling you to snooze your alarm or take a night off, tell that voice to stop it because you have very important work to do to further and benefit yourself and your life.

Find a healthy support system

It's incredibly important that you find or obtain a healthy support system that allows you to grow and achieve and have access to your goals and one that further empowers or assists you with achieving these tasks. Impossible goals can be isolating, so you want to make sure you have a support system that understands what you are trying to achieve. A support team will typically include a mentor, professional groups and friends who share similar goals or interests.

Never give up or quit

There will be times when you will want to quit or stop your endeavors or pursuits. it is extremely important to not stop doing what you are doing and to push forward and move forward. It's important to laugh through the tears for you might even find yourself wanting to quit or end the pursuit you are attempting to excel at. You shouldn't ever allow yourself to give up or leave the situation for your task is to achieve the goal and it's something that is very capable of committing so what better person to do than your own self?

Chapter 8

The Souled Being Within

Our souls are the gateways to our inner self, and also to our higher selves and are the blessed pathways to greater and more elevated levels of bliss and consciousness. The being we are within isn't of material nature. It isn't the flesh and bones that make up our existence as humans on this physical plane. The beings we are within, are greater elements of the souls that we possess within ourselves, and these are the greater creatures we were meant to be and who we truly are within ourselves. We aren't creations that lack a soul, on the contrary we do have a soul within us. There are many theories and perspectives within religious belief systems and schools of thought that have opinions on the concept of whether or not a soul exists within a human being or living beings.

The soul can be defined as the immaterial aspect or essence of a human being, that which defines individuality and humanity, and is usually synonymous with the mind or the self. In theology, the soul is further defined as that part of the individual which partakes of divinity and often is considered to survive the death of the body. The soul is the light essence of a human's being, and the part of the person that makes up ethereal presence within a person and is usually light, and energy, as opposed to the material that a human's physical body is. The soul is perfection in all of its presence and contains the qualities of absolute truth, absolute consciousness, and bliss energy. The soul is beyond the three basic components, however the rest of our consciousness such as the physical and mental body are made up of it.

The soul is a philosophical and often religious concept representing the eternal, immaterial essence or core of an individual. It is believed by some to be the seat of consciousness, identity, and the source of one's unique character. Different cultures and religions have varying perspectives on the nature of the soul, with interpretations ranging from reincarnation to an afterlife. The concept of the soul is often intertwined with notions of spirituality and personal transcendence.

Consciousness refers to an individual's awareness and perception of both the external world and their own internal thoughts, feelings, and experiences. It involves the ability to perceive, think, and have subjective experiences. The nature of consciousness is a complex topic that has intrigued philosophers, scientists, and scholars for centuries, and it remains a subject of ongoing exploration and study. Understanding consciousness involves delving into questions about self-awareness, perception, and the neural processes that give rise to our conscious experiences.

The relationship between the soul and spirit is often shaped by individual beliefs and perspectives. In various philosophical and religious traditions. The soul is associated with an individual's consciousness and essence, and even personal identity. It is considered the unchanging, eternal core that exists throughout one's existence.

The spirit is more of a dynamic and transcendent force that connects individuals to a universal energy or divine presence. The spirit is the animating force that breathes the life force into a soul. The soul is often viewed as the individual's unique essence, while spirit is seen as a universal, connecting force that may influence or guide the soul. These concepts vary across different cultural and religious perspectives.

Spirituality is a deeply personal and subjective concept that involves a sense of connection to something greater than oneself. It often encompasses a search for meaning, purpose, and understanding of one's existence. Spirituality can be expressed through religious beliefs, practices, or through a more individualistic exploration of personal values, inner peace, and a connection to the transcendent or sacred. It is a broad and diverse concept, with individuals finding spiritual fulfillment in various ways.

It is important that we encompass the concepts of what spirituality entails and examine the various aspects of the soul, for the soul exists within our mortal bodies. portion of the soul and try to examine the various aspects that the soul possesses within our mortal bodies.

The soul is the essence of our body and the portion that holds the key to our morality, and our mortality for the soul is actually immortal and it does not die. It lives on it moves into different bodies.

The soul is a beautiful facet of ourselves and our spiritual and energy body. The soul harnesses and harbors no thoughts and feelings. It is full of light, energy and love and bliss energy, but there are various parts of it that encompass the entire body. This is what many philosophers believed or felt.

Plato's perception of the soul

The famous Greek thinker Plato believed the soul consisted of three parts. Plato believed that the soul was the source of life and of the mind. He also believed the soul was the bearer of moral properties of a person and that it was also the thinking portion of a person. He felt that after death, the soul was able to think and existed after a person passed from this world.

Plato felt the soul consisted of three major parts

The appetites which include all of our desires for various pleasures, comforts, physical satisfactions, and bodily ease. Plato felt that many of these appetites can be in conflict with each other.

The spirited part is the part that gets angry when it perceives an injustice being done. This is the part of us that loves to face and overcome great challenges, the part that can steel itself to adversity, and that loves victory, winning, challenge, and honor and encompasses emotions such as courage, anger, and ambition. This aspect of the soul causes people to defend their beliefs, seek nobility and honor, and display determination in the face of challenges. This part of the soul holds immense energy and power. This element of the soul is represented by the noble white horse on the right.

The third part of the soul is the rational mind. This is the part of us that thinks, analyzes, looks ahead, attempts to display rationality, and tries to gauge what is best overall. This part of the soul seeks truth and reason. This is the highest and most divine aspect of the soul. It is associated with reason, intellect, and integrity.

According to Plato, the three parts of the soul interact in a very hierarchical manner. The mind or rational portion should govern and guide the spirited and appetitive parts making sure that reason and wisdom prevail over all lower emotions and desires.

Plato's concept of the soul consisted of the logos, which is located in the head and is related to reason, the thymos which is located near the chest region, and which is consistent with spirit, and the eros which is located in the stomach and is connected to one's desires. Plato believed that the soul was a self-mover and it is the soul which gives life to the body.

Aristotle's perception of the soul

Aristotle felt that the soul is the form or essence of a living being and is responsible for its development and functioning. Aristotle, just like his teacher Plato, categorized the soul into three important parts: the vegetative soul- which is responsible for growth and reproduction, the sensitive soul- which is responsible for desire and perception, and the rational soul, which is responsible for reason and intellect.

Aristotle believed that the vegetative soul is responsible for basic life functions such as growth, nutrition, and reproduction in living organisms. It is associated with plants and animals and does contain consciousness. He perceived the vegetative soul as the foundational part of the soul, and it serves as a basis for the rational and sensitive souls.

The other parts of the soul basically build upon and incorporate high functions that the vegetative soul does not possess such as cognitive abilities and sensory perception.

The sensitive soul is responsible for perception and sensation. It is a part of animals and humans and allows creatures to have awareness of the environment, and experience emotions.

Aristotle too felt like the rational soul was the highest and most distinctive part of the soul. It is associated with the notion for intellect, reason and the ability to contemplate concepts. Aristotle felt it is this rational aspect that causes distinguishes humans from other living creatures. He felt it enabled humans to be abstract thinkers, think and reason philosophically, and have free will.

Aristotle viewed the sensitive soul as a precursor to the rational soul. He felt the the sensitive soul provided a foundation for sensory experience which is then used by the rational soul for higher functions such as intellect and reasoning. The rational soul builds upon the capacities of the sensitive soul.

Aristotle identifies soul with form, and body with matter. He assumes that to have a soul is to have the functional properties that are the form, and the relation of the soul to the body is the relation of the form to matter, and of actuality of potentiality.

The Christian perception of the soul

According to the Christian point of view, and soul creationism, God creates each individual soul directly, either at the moment of conception or at some later time. According to traducianism, the soul comes from the parents by natural generation. According to the preexistence theory, the soul exists before the moment of conception. There have been differing thoughts regarding whether embryos have souls from conception, or whether there is a point between conception and birth where the fetus acquires a soul or personhood.

Christians believe the soul continues its existence immediately after death. Most believe it will do so consciously. At the point of death, God will determine the soul's ultimate fate-eternal punishment or eternal happiness.

The soul is believed to be the eternal and spiritual essence of a person that is created by God and lives after death. The soul in Christianity is perceived as the head of a person's consciousness, emotions and moral nature. The soul is the key and gateway to a person's spiritual and moral beliefs.

Christianity perceives the body and soul as connected but being different elements. The body is the physical vessel that houses a person's soul during a person's earthly life. At death, the soul separates from the body and exists in the afterlife. Within Christianity, the soul is an extremely important part of the body, and it does exist after a person's physical body doesn't.

Islamic perception of the soul

Within Islam, the soul is believed to be a spiritual element created by Allah (God). It is seen as the essence of a person that is breathed into the body at the time of conception. The soul is the source of consciousness, morality, intellect and free will. After death, the soul still continues to exist and undergoes a waiting period until it is time for the day of judgment to come.

Within Islam, there are different beliefs and interpretations regarding the nature and journey of the soul. There might be varying and different beliefs with regards to what happens to the soul after death, and its relationship with the body. These differences are brought upon by various schools of thought or even cultural beliefs.

Buddhist perception of the soul

The Buddha teaches that what we call ego, self, soul, etc are only conventional terms that do not refer to any real, independent entity. According to Buddhism there is no reason to believe that there is an eternal soul that comes from heaven or that is created by itself and that will transmigrate or proceed straight away either to heaven or hell after death. Buddhists cannot accept that there is anything either in this world or any other world that is eternal or unchangeable.

In Buddhism, the concept of the soul is taught as 'no-self' or 'annata', which means there is no permanent unchanging soul or self. Buddhism believes in a changing, interconnected steam of consciousness called annata.

The Buddha said that all phenomena are conditioned, and all conditioned phenomena are impermanent. We are made up of many parts and are constantly changing. Buddhism does state that we have a nature that transcends conditioned or material existence. This is considered buddhanature- the open expanse of awakeness in which all good qualities reside.

The soul consists of pure light energy, and it encompasses our very core, as well as the entire portion of our bodies. It is the part of the body that is overtly hidden, and yet it seems to encompass a great portion of our thinking and is the basis for many spiritual, religious and philosophical theories out there. The soul may be hidden, but it is a huge part of our lives and not only makes up most of our bodies, but within the soul lies many hidden secrets of our past lives and where we as individuals originated from.

The soul might seem like a basic simplistic creation, but within it lies the many truths and secrets of our pasts as who we are and who we once were. Within the soul lies the akashic records. What are the akashic records? The akashic records are a hidden collection of records which manifest from the past and throughout lifetimes and worlds and various realms and which explain to us the hidden truths of our past and have a plethora of many hidden and untold stories of our lives and every person and animal's life.

The soul is clearly immortal and does not die. It lives on and remains intact and moves into different lifetimes and various worlds for each human or being that is harbors throughout. It is the most important aspect of our lives and our bodies and holds within it many special keys and secrets not only to our world, but the truths about the planet and the world in general.

Chapter 9

The Beauty Of Compassion

Compassion is a beautiful, wonderful, amazing concept to possess and to have within oneself and life and it is the wonder of having compassion that can allow others to live and breathe a life of beauty, ecstasy, and true spirituality. What is compassion? Compassion can be defined as a deep feeling of empathy and concern for the suffering of others. It involves recognizing the pain or difficulties someone is experiencing and having a genuine desire to alleviate their suffering and help allow them to have a better sense of well-being. Compassion can be kindness, understanding, and support.

Compassion can be compared to having empathy, but it is deeper than empathy for it involves having a deep care for those who are in need of help or just caring in general for others or having a strong concern for the plight of other living beings.

The Buddha, Siddhartha Gautama taught that compassion is a central virtue and a key aspect of spiritual development. He emphasized the importance of showing kindness, empathy and goodness towards all beings and living creations as it leads to liberation from suffering.

He also believed that compassion is a fundamental aspect of spiritual development and is the path to true enlightenment. Buddha felt that compassion was about the understanding of the suffering of others and having the desire to eliminate it. He encouraged others to practice kindness and to treat all creatures with goodness, empathy, and respect. By being compassionate, a person can overcome being selfish, and gain a deep sense of being connected with all beings.

There are many examples of compassion in the world. There are many benefits of practicing compassion for it can create positive relationships, enhance well-being, relieve stress, elevate happiness, and improve mental and emotional health. It also allows a person to exercise a sense of goodness and duty to one another and allows someone to feel better about themselves as a person and allows one to do good and spread good to others and allow that to snowball a situation or scenario. Those who practice compassion are contributing to a happier and better society as a whole.

There are many ways a person can increase or cultivate compassion in their everyday lives.

1. Be a kind person and do kind deeds to others

Be a good person and engage in kind acts towards people in your neighborhood, community and towards your friends and family as well.

2. Be empathetic

Do your best to understand other people's feelings and emotions and try to figure out why they feel the way they do feel. This is extremely important because it will allow you to put yourself in other people's shoes and be a more caring and good person and understanding other people's perspectives will allow your levels of kindness and compassion to skyrocket.

3. Hang around like-minded and compassionate people

People learn from others. It's important to be around kind, caring, and compassionate good people so that you can learn from each other and grow within the compassion you do possess.

4. Reflect on being like others

Understand the concept that all beings are connected and feel in a similar way, and that we all share the same morals and values. All creatures share a desire for happiness and freedom from pain or suffering.

Self-compassion

Practicing self-compassion is very important for harnessing compassion for others. When we are kind to ourselves, we develop a great capacity and empathy to love and harbor that same kindness and love towards others too. By loving ourselves, we learn the concept of how to love and be kind and can spread that kindness, goodness, and love to others. If we don't practice loving ourselves first and foremost, then we risk the chance of not being able to fully love others or understand what the concept of love and compassion truly are.

By recognizing our own issues and treating ourselves with goodness and compassion, we become more attuned and have a greater understanding of the needs of others and this encourages a deeper understanding of the concept of compassion. Self-compassion also allows us to harbor and understand the idea of being compassionate towards everyone equally and allows our sense of compassion to grow and exponentiate.

Self-compassion can lead to greater compassion for others overall and allows us to understand common humanity. When we are compassionate towards ourselves, we understand that we are not the only ones who experience difficulties. We learn to embrace our faults, issues, and practice only kindness and caring towards ourselves. This understanding lets us empathize with other people's plights and struggles and lets us respond to those situations through the lens of compassion, love, and light and not of judgments or any form of wickedness.

Self-compassion allows us to stop judging or criticizing others or being harsh on ourselves or anyone. By accepting ourselves, we in fact become less inclined to judge or put others down or perceive their situations as being difficult or complicated, rather we become less inclined to judge or criticize others. We then harbor a more non-judgmental and non-critical attitude towards others.

Self-compassion allows us to cope with our own issues and situation and lets us develop emotional resilience. This special form of resilience lets us be more caring, kind and understanding of other people's situations and plights, and allows us to be there for others and offer support for them.

When we treat ourselves with kindness and compassion, we become role models for others. By showing self-compassion, we encourage others to cultivate compassion for themselves and for others as well.

Within spirituality, compassion is the gateway to harmony, peace, bliss and goodness.

Compassion allows you the opportunity to love, live, laugh and be full of joy beauty and wondrous elation. It allows you to put yourself in other people's shoes and situation and lets you discover the truth with regards to how people may feel about particular situations and circumstances. Compassion allows you to develop a deeper understanding and love of many different aspects and elements in life and lets you be the greater person you were meant to be. It is a key and essential element of being a more spiritual person with a deeper understanding of many key elements in life. You were meant to be a compassionate, understanding, and caring person not one full of hatred, confusion, lack of care or strife.

Practicing compassion can have numerous health benefits as well. It can increase happiness, reduce stress, allow improvement in relationships, and can allow someone to feel a greater sense of purpose in life. Compassion can let a person's social environment be better in general as well and thrive as cultivating compassion can allow a person more joy and happiness in general, and one can gain a greater sense of happiness within interpersonal scenarios and interactions.

The Buddha taught us to practice compassion and to be kind to others as did other religious teachers such as Prophet Muhammed and Jesus of Nazareth. Most religious figures taught the concept of compassion because it builds our strengths, integrity and our characters and allows us to be better people overall and lets us practice patience and lets us harness these positive and beneficial qualities.

There are numerous ways to cultivate and engage in compassionate acts or the concept of compassion. Being kind, practicing empathy, volunteering, being introspective, and listening to others allows one to engage in acts of compassion. Meditation is another key element that allows someone to further enhance their sense of compassion.

One major benefit of compassion is that it allows us to understand those who suffer and the concept of suffering in an elevated form. Once you awaken spiritually and compassion becomes important to a person, they will have a heightened understanding of the concept of compassion and love every element of it and will want to become more compassionate especially towards those who are down or suffering and this is an extremely important part of being a compassionate person within the ideation of spirituality.

This is one of the most important elements of becoming a more spiritual person overall- the transformation takes place and you will become and grow into a much greater and compassionate person and learn how to elevate your love and compassion for the plight of others, which you will also learn is the most important element and concept on this planet- to aid those who are in need of help or those who are suffering.

We should be against anything that causes harm or suffering to others as spiritual and human beings and this is a huge understanding you will have and learn- the extreme importance of helping those who are down and who are in need of your help or the help of others. That is one of the key elements and beauty of being a compassionate wonderful and amazing spiritual person and one of the few amazing things the concept of compassion within spirituality and in general can allow a person to gain.

Chapter 10

SPIRITUAL HEALING

Spiritual healing is comprised of many various effective methods that can assist and allow someone to become healed and to grow spiritually and morally in all sorts of amazing and gracious ways. People of all kinds are in dire need of spiritual healing on all levels. Healing is an extremely important part of being a spiritual person and practitioners can gain greater insight into being more whole and one with their own techniques, and those who are in need of spiritual healing can become more learned on the various techniques that are used to heal someone and need to know the effectiveness by which specific modalities yield and what can be the best healing methods out there for someone.

Different types of spiritual healing

Spiritual healing is an extremely important and fundamental asset for those out there who are going through spiritual crisis, crisis of any form, have become diseased in any form, have leakages in their chakras or energy body, are in need of patching up holes in their energy body, or who need to help with spiritual awakening or are in need of assistance with raising their vibration and better connecting with their spiritual self or spirit body. There are many varying means by which a person can become healed spiritually or by which a practitioner can heal his or her clients. A person can become spiritually healed by teachers/healers, objects, herbal or medicinal remedies, plants/nature, meditation, reiki, light energy, energy work, and stones/crystals.

Spiritual healing is a holistic approach that aims to restore balance and harmony to a person's mind, body, and spirit. It often involves practices such as meditation, prayer, energy healing, and mindfulness to promote well-being and address emotional or spiritual distress. There are many varying kinds of spiritual healing that exist out there from inanimate object healing to finding healers, and it can take on many different forms and modalities.

Spiritual healing can take various forms, including:

Meditation: Focusing the mind to achieve a sense of peace and inner balance.

Prayer: Seeking divine intervention or guidance for healing.

Energy Healing: Practices like Reiki, where practitioners channel energy to promote healing.

Mindfulness: Cultivating awareness of the present moment to reduce stress and enhance well-being.

Yoga: Combining physical postures, breath control, and meditation for holistic well-being.

Chanting and Affirmations: Using positive words or sounds to shift energy and mindset.

Connecting with Nature: Finding solace and healing through a connection with the natural world.

Spiritual Counseling: Seeking guidance from a spiritual leader or counselor.

These modes can be complementary to conventional medical treatments, focusing on the spiritual aspect of health and healing.

Inanimate objects

Inanimate objects can be used very effectively for various modalities of healing. These objects can be crystals, amulets, stones, holy ash, holy water, colors, incense sticks, ghee lamp, cow's urine, and voices or written statements made by saints. The basic principle of this mode of healing is that by raising the basic principle of positivity of the object at hand, and by raising the spiritual purity of the affected area, we can reduce the negative energy that affects a person. The increased spiritual purity then works through a combination of the absolute cosmic principles to bring about some form of healing process.

What is Energy Healing?

Energy healing is the process of restoring balance and wellness to your energy field. It is based on the interconnectedness of all life, and the belief that energy flows through and surrounds us all. When our energy is disrupted or blocked, it can lead to physical, emotional, or spiritual disharmony.

Energy healing is a holistic practice that is rooted in balancing the body's energy system properly and with effective practices and techniques. It is based on the concept that imbalances or issues in the energy flow can lead to emotional, physical or spiritual health concerns and ailments.

Energy healing has begun through ancient forms of medicine, such as traditional Chinese medicine and Ayurveda which is practiced in India. The concept of Traditional Chinese medicine is that a vital energy force, known as "qi," surges throughout the body. When there is an imbalance of qi, disease and illness may result.

Similarly, Ayurveda, which originated in India more than 3,000 years ago, is a system of medicine based on the principle that disease is caused by an imbalance or stress in a person's consciousness. The vital energy concept in Ayurveda is called "prana" and has similarities to qi in Chinese medicine.

The consensual goal in both healing modalities is to support the body to achieve balance and realign your energy to find healing. This is done with a number of health and energy healing tools.

Energy healing can be used to address a variety of issues, including:

- Physical pain
- Emotional stress or anxiety
- Relationship problems
- Spiritual blockages or stagnation

Different Types of Energy Healing

There are many types of energy healing modalities, each with its own unique approach and benefits. Depending on your needs and intentions, some may be more aligned to your individual energy system than others. Energy healing is one of the more effective techniques of ridding a person of unwanted negative energies, spiritual blockages, dealing with spiritual crisis and for allowing a person to restore or balance their energetic and spiritual body and allowing everything to become balanced and whole once again.

Reiki

Reiki is a Japanese technique that involves the transfer of healing energy from a practitioner to a recipient. The word "Reiki" is derived from the words "rei" which means universal, or spiritual and "ki", which is the life force energy. It is believed that a person's "ki" can become depleted or imbalanced which leads to emotional, physical, or spiritual issues.

Reiki is a very popular and well-known healing technique that uses universal energy to restore balance and harmony. The practitioner directs this energy to where it is needed most by placing their hands near or on the body. Recipients may feel the release of stuck emotions, relaxation, and peace during a session. Reiki is an incredibly effective known energy healing technique which many practitioners tend to use and it works in a very effective way to get rid of unwanted energies, blockages, and allows a person to feel more relaxed, whole, free and assists with various functions in the body.

It is often used as a complementary therapy to conventional medicine to support overall well-being and assist the body's natural healing process.

Acupuncture

Acupuncture is a practice that uses energy pathways, called meridians, to restore balance and harmony. The belief is that by inserting needles into specific points along these meridians, practitioners can unblock any stagnation and restore the flow of health and wellness.

The goal of acupuncture is to restore the balance of this energy and to stimulate the body's natural healing abilities. When needles are inserted into specific points in the body, blockages and imbalances can be removed and the body can be restored to full harmony. Acupunture can treat pain, respiratory issues, and digestive problems. It can also be used for relaxation and overall well-being.

Massage

Massage is one of the oldest and most common forms of energy healing. The therapist uses their hands to move energy around your body. This can help promote relaxation, improve blood and lymphatic circulation. Massage is a therapeutic technique that manipulates the body's soft tissues along with the muscles, tendons, ligaments, and fascia to promote relaxation, and reduce pain. There are various types of massages including Swedish massage, deep tissue massage, sports massage, trigger point massage and Thai massage, which all offer extreme benefits to the overall well-being of a person's body.

Massage offers many health benefits such as pain relief, stress reduction, improved circulation, and extra relaxation.

Reflexology

Reflexology is a type of massage that uses pressure points on the feet, hands, and ears to promote healing. Reflexologists believe that these pressure points correspond to different parts of the body. By massaging or applying pressure to these points, we can encourage energy to flow freely and restore balance. Reflexology states that these reflex points are connected to various parts of the body through energy channels. When these points are stimulated, the corresponding body parts can be influenced in a positive way, and there is an increase in relaxation, stress reduction, and supporting overall health and well-being.

Craniosacral Therapy

Craniosacral therapy is a light touch treatment that uses gentle hands-on techniques to examine the movement of fluids in and around the central nervous system. This therapy can help relieve stress, tension headaches, and neck pain. Craniosacral therapy is also known to help restore balance and wellness after traumatic injuries.

It enhances the body's natural healing abilities and promotes overall well-being by releasing imbalances in the system. It can be used to address conditions such as chronic pain, headaches, migraines, TMJ dysfunction and musculoskeletal concerns.

Yoga

Yoga is an ancient healing modality that uses movement, meditation, and the chakra system to support healing and well-being. Some popular styles of yoga that focus on energy healing include Kundalini, Iyengar, and Vinyasa. It originated in ancient India and has been passed down through generations. It is comprised of physical postures (asanas), breathing exercises (pranayama), meditation and other principles. The concept of yoga is about uniting the mind, body, and spirit, promoting overall well-being and inner goodness. Yoga offers many health benefits such as strength, balance, relaxation, and improved flexibility. It can also reduce stress and enhance mental clarity. Yoga is a very versatile art and can be changed to fit individual needs.

Qi Gong

Qi Gong is a Chinese practice that combines movement, breath control, and meditation to cultivate and balance the body's important vital energy known as 'qi' or 'chi.' Qi Gong has its roots in Traditional Chinese medicine and Taoism. It is a system of energy healing that uses movement, breathwork, and visualization to open and balance the energy pathways in the body. Qi Gong aims to improve health and help relieve stress, anxiety, and pain.

Qi Gong exercises usually involve flowing movements, deep breathing techniques, and focuses intention. It promotes the flow of "qi" throughout the body, enhances overall health, and strengthens the body's energy system. It supports and improves emotional balance, physical fitness, and reduces stress overall.

Ecstatic Dance

This is a new form of energy healing. Ecstatic dance uses movement and music to open the body, mind, and spirit. During an ecstatic dance session, participants move freely to express their emotions and connect with their inner power. This type of dance is thought to release blocked energy, clear the mind, and boost self-confidence.

Sound Healing

Sound healing is a holistic practice that uses sound and vibration to restore balance and harmony in the body. By listening to certain sounds or music, you can stimulate different parts of the body, promote relaxation, and improve mental clarity. It involves the use of sound tools as such singing bowls, tuning forks, gongs, and the human voice to create harmonious sounds for various types of healing.

These sounds are meant to resonate with the body and mind and help restore balance and harmony within a person. It Is often used with other healing modalities and practices.

Shamanic Healing

Shamanic healing uses plant medicines and spiritual ceremonies to restore balance to the body, mind, and spirit. Shamanic healers use tools like the drum, prayers, and rituals to help restore energy levels and health. Shamanic healing addresses mental, emotional, and spiritual imbalances as well. It aims to restore harmony, promote personal growth, and helps reconnect individuals with their true selves. It is rooted in cultural traditions and expects to be approached with great understanding and respect.

Possible Benefits of Energy Healing

There are many various important benefits that come with energy healing.

Some data suggests some forms of energy healing, including reiki, acupuncture, qigong, and reflexology may come with several health benefits, such as pain relief, improved depression and anxiety, and enhanced overall well-being. It also helps to balance the body's energy flow, enhance the body's natural healing abilities, and provide a sense of emotional and spiritual harmony and balance overall, and improve depression and anxiety symptoms.

Energy healing may improve mood and even helps with symptoms of depression and anxiety, according to many different studies. A review in 2017 of various studies determined that Reiki was more effective than a placebo in reducing depression and anxiety and improving an overall quality of life. Scientific studies done in 2021 involved more than 1200 adolescents and determined that qigong reduced depression and anxiety in teens effectively. Energy healing techniques also promote deep relaxation which helps with an overall sense of well-being.

Currently, energy healing is being studied in patients who receive cancer therapy to determine if it can improve the quality of life, boost the immune system, or reduce the side effects of cancer. A study showed that women with breast cancer who received reflexology treatments, showed improvement in various symptoms and overall physical functioning. Reiki and other energy healing modalities are becoming more common for hospital patients as well.

There is limited scientific evidence on the study of energy healing, though the studies that have been done suggest many potential and important life-long benefits. More research is necessary to understand its mechanisms and the manner in which energy healing modalities tend to work. It is often an alternative therapy and can be used in conjunction with other traditional medicines and healing therapies, and its effectiveness varies from person to person.

Chapter 11

Chakra Cleansing and Healing

The chakras are an extremely important element in the concept of spirituality. The chakras are the energy or energetic systems that are present within a human being. A chakra is a concept in Hindu and Buddhist religious belief systems that refer to energy centers in the body. There are seven main chakras in the body that correspond to different aspects of physical, emotional, and spiritual well-being.

The word chakra can be traced back to 600 BC where chakras were first mentioned as psychic focal points of consciousness in the Indian

Upanishads which are historical Hindu texts. The first concept of chakras first came about in Hinduism and Tantric Buddhism. It was then introduced in the Vedas and Yoga Sutras.

Today, the concept of chakra is very popular among the New Age Movement in the West.

The chakras are located from the spine to the base of the spine to the crown of the head. They are associated with qualities and specific functions such as creativity, grounding, personal power, love, communication, intuition, and spiritual connection. It is like a spinning wheel or vortex of energy that is present within the energy body of a person located in the middle of the body down along the spine.

Yogic beliefs speak of seven chakras, however, there are really 114 chakras with 72,000 Nadis or energy channels in the body. 112 chakras are in the physical structure of the body and the other two are on the outer plane.

Out of 114 chakras, 86 are micro chakras which are considered to be acupuncture points on the body. 21 are minor chakras that work with the major chakras and are distributed throughout the body. The last 7 are considered the major chakras- 5 lie along the spinal column, one is located on the forehead, and one is located over the head outside of the body.

Each chakra has a specific role, energy frequency, symbol and is identified by a unique color. Each one is connected to various organs and glands within the body to channel the energy in the form of 'prana' through Nadis or special channels.

It is important to balance and align these chakras and cleanse them out through practices such as yoga, meditation, and energy healing in order to create harmony and overall well-being within a person.

The Root Chakra

The Root Chakra is red in color and is located in the base of the spine.

Function: grounding, security, survival, foundation of your physical and emotional well-being.

When the Root Chakra is properly aligned, a person will feel grounded and secure.

An imbalance in the root chakra can bring about fear, anxiety, feeling ungrounded, disconnected. A blocked Root Chakra can manifest as issues such as constipation, arthritis, and bladder or colon problems.

Sacral Chakra

The Sacral Chakra is orange colored, and is located below the belly button

Function: creativity, sensuality, pleasure, emotional expression, relationships

An imbalance in the sacral chakra can cause someone to have difficulty expressing emotions, lack of creativity, intimacy issues. This chakra is connected to our feelings of self-worth around pleasure, creativity and sexuality.

Solar Plexus Chakra

This chakra is yellow in color and it is located above the navel.

Function: personal power, confidence, self-esteem, willpower, digestion

Someone with imbalance in the Solar Plexus Chakra will have a lack of self-confidence, low self-worth, and difficulty making decisions.

Heart Chakra

The Heart Chakra is green and is located in the center of the chest.

Function: love, compassion, empathy, forgiveness, self-acceptance

The Heart Chakra bridges the gap between our upper and lower chakras because it's the middle of the seven chakras. It represents our ability to love and connect to others.

When the Heart Chakra is out of alignment, it can make us feel insecure, lonely and isolated. An imbalance in the heart chakra can cause difficulty giving or receiving love, emotional walls, bitterness and grief.

Throat Chakra

The Throat Chakra is blue in color and is located in the throat.

Function: communication, self-expression, truthfulness, creativity

When a person's Throat Chakra is balanced and aligned, they will speak and listen with compassion and confidence. They know they are being true to their own selves. Someone with imbalance in the throat chakra will have difficulty communicating, shyness, fear of speaking up, and creative blocks.

Third Eye Chakra

This chakra is indigo in color and is located between the eyes on the forehead and Is also known as the brow chakra.

Function: intuition, insight, wisdom, imagination, seeing beyond the physical

When open and aligned, people will be able to follow their intuition and witness the big picture.

Blockages can manifest as headaches, issues with concentration, and hearing problems. An imbalance in the third eye chakra can result in lack of clarity, difficulty trusting one's intuition, and closed mindedness.

Crown Chakra

This chakra is located at the crown of the head and is white or violet in color

Function: spirituality, connection to the universe, oneness, enlightenment

The Crown Chakra is linked to every other chakra and affects all of those organs as well as the brain and nervous system. When the crown chakra is aligned and open, it keeps all the other chakras open and can bring a person bliss and enlightenment.

An imbalance in this chakra can cause one to feel disconnected, lack of meaning or purpose, and spiritual emptiness.

How to cleanse the chakras

There are many ways to cleanse the chakras and many of them involve specific visualizations which allow you to cleanse the chakras out and use different methods or even abilities to do this. You can also go to a healer to do this and they using their abilities, will be able to perform a chakra cleanse on you.

It is important to make sure that the chakras are constantly cleansed out at least twice a year simply because you want to make sure that the chakras have no issues within them or you will have a host of mental and physical ailments present. In the chakra system, blockages may pop up every now and then, and these patterns have specific concepts and there are many various recommended treatments for them.

It is important to make sure that a person's chakras are fully cleansed to make sure that everything is going well energetically and spiritually within a person's energy body system. There are various techniques used to unblock chakras and cleanse them out.

Mantras

Mantras are short repetitions or sayings that are used during yoga practice or while practicing spiritual meditation. It can act as a form of sound healing and can help restore your energy fields.

Chakra meditation

A chakra meditation can be a very effective technique and involves bringing attention to your chakras and focusing on your awareness. There are various ways of doing a chakra meditation.

Yoga

Movement can be a very effective way of releasing a blocked chakra or assisting with getting rid of the blockage. Yoga encouarges the flow of energy back into your body.

Essential Oils

Using essential oils is a wonderful way to rebalance a person's chakras. Using the oils at home is a way to unblock chakras

Nutrition

Incorporating specific foods in your diet can help you clear your energy system. Each chakra does correlate with specific foods so bringing the right foods into every meal can assist with rebalancing the chakra system.

Take deep breaths

Taking deep breaths can be an effective way of restoring your chakras to their natural and original states. If you inhale, direct energy to the chakras, and as you exhale allow awareness into it.

Visualization techniques

There are visualization techniques where you will need to visualize the chakra and all the dirt within it and begin to envision cleansing out the chakra energetically and mentally. This is a very effective way of cleansing out a chakra.

Chakras have states of activeness. When the energy or prana within a chakra is spinning at a higher rate than the normal one, the chakra is said to be in an overactive state. You will often feel the energy then flow through the corresponding organs of the overactive chakra.

When energy spins at the normal rate then the chakra is said to be in a balanced state. And when prana or energy spins slower than usual due to lack of physical activity, the chakra is then known to be underactive. If a chakra gets blocked, it can cause illness and other issues that may be physical or behavioral.

How to balance and heal the Root Chakra

Connect yourself with earthly elements

Channel your energy into doing hobbies such as gardening or walking

By chanting the sound "Lam" which is a specific mantra

By eating red colored root vegetables such as carrots, potatoes, radish, tomatoes, cherries, strawberries.

By wearing stones or gems such as black tourmaline, bloodstone and other stones that help stimulate the chakra

How to balance and heal the Sacral Chakra

Direct the overactive energy of in a nearby chakra. You will need to leave the normal pleasures in life and be more in tune with natural ideas and things.

Do any action only if it's beneficial or healthy for you

Recite the sound "Vam" while meditating

Keep yourself close to water and water bodies can help level the low energy since the element of Sacral Chakra is water

Gems such as Citrine, Orange Calcite, and Coral Calcite can help bring up the level of the Sacral Chakra energy

How to balance and heal the Solar Plexus Chakra

Show compassion and empathy for others and yourself

Give more for yourself and become more self-aware of your actions

Your actions need to be very positive and only affect people positively

Chant the word "Ram" to restore this chakra to its original energized state

Yellow colored foods tend to help stimulate the solar plexus chakra. You can add turmeric and eat yellow-colored fruits and vegetables. Add flax seeds and rice to boost this chakra.

Stones that help stimulate this chakra are Citrine, Amber, Yellow Jasper, and Yellow Tourmaline

How to balance and heal the Heart Chakra

Go out in nature more often

It's important to let go and to love yourself

Do what you are interested in doing

Stay kind and compassionate towards others

Consume green food and hang out in places full of greenery and surround yourself with this color

Recite the chant of "Yum" while meditating to the level of heart chakra

Wear stones and gems that help enhance and restore the heart chakra such as Malachite, Epidote, and Chrysoprase.

How to balance and heal the Throat Chakra

Learn to listen more to others and speak less

Practice being more patient

Since blue is the color of the throat chakra, stay near the blue sky or the ocean

Get involved in art and creative matters more often

Chant the Mantra Hum/Ham while meditating

Wear specific blue stones and gems such as Azurite, Lapis, Turquoise, Lazuli and Aquamarine

How to balance and heal the Third-Eye Chakra

Connect yourself to the ground, and become more grounded

Work on the lower level chakras such as the Heart, Throat and Sacral

Eat very healthy and add blueberries, raspberries, grapes and wine to your diet

Chant the sound Om/Aum while meditating

Wear Third-Eye Chakra gems and stones such as indigo Kyanite, Quartz, and Tanzanite to bring this chakra to its balanced and healed state

How to balance and heal the Crown Chakra

Live in a state of thanks and help others with the things that you do possess

Recite the mantra Om/Aum while meditating

Eat foods such as Sage, Myrrh, and Copal to restore the proper energy levels

Wear Kyanite to enhance the energy level of the Crown Chakra

Chakras are necessary energy points in the body of a human being. When your chakras are properly aligned and at their normal energy levels then a person will feel at their best and very healthy and well. When there are imbalances in the Chakras, then problems can arise and a person can feel tired, lethargic and even depressed.

It is important to make sure that the chakras are working properly and that a person is at their healthiest and doing well with regards to these chakras. Sometimes, it is necessary to incorporate energetic and nutritional care in order to make sure that the chakras are working at their best. Many physical ailments are said to be healed by opening up and healing the chakras and making sure they are aligned and healthy.

Chapter 12

Prayer and Peace

Prayer is one of the first and foremost important elements within the concept of spirituality. Prayer is a form of communication with a higher power or deity, and is often used for expressing gratitude, seeking guidance, or making requests. It can take various forms, such as spoken words, thoughts, or rituals. It is a key method and manner by which spiritual practices can be held through and it can take on many various forms.

Prayer can have incredibly positive effects on mental and emotional well-being. It can provide a sense of comfort, hope, and connection with the divine or a higher power, reducing stress and promoting feelings of peace and relaxation. It may also help individuals cope with challenges and find meaning in difficult situations.

Prayer can be very beneficial for people of all religious or spiritual beliefs. It can be used and practiced by people of all religious backgrounds and belief systems and is not limited to any particular school of thought. Different schools of thought and belief systems have various modes of prayer; however, different religious systems have their own perspective and perception on what the concept of prayer is and how it can be used to help guide the masses, and to channel God and higher powers in order to gain some form of satisfaction or wish that a person may have or need. It is a personal practice that can provide comfort, reflection, and a sense of connection with something greater, regardless of specific beliefs or traditions. The form and content of prayer may vary, but the underlying intention of seeking solace or guidance remains universal.

The concept of prayer can be found within many different religious belief systems and within many different spiritual practices that exist out there. Prayer is utilized to effectively channel a higher power or God and through prayer you're able to talk to God make requests for specific wishes or just ask for overall well-being. There are many things that prayer does overall and many aspects that take place when a person is performing a prayer depending on what kind of ritual they are performing.

There are hundreds of types of prayers that can be done, and the benefit of these prayers can be numerous in nature. Prayer is the gateway to greater peace and harmony within a person's inner self and within their life as well.

If a person wants to gain access to eternal peace and happiness, then they need to utilize the beauty and harmony of prayer, for prayer will give them the peace they so deserve and need in order to gain a greater understanding of spiritual concepts and all that is within the elements of spiritual nature.

Prayer can be very important for people because it provides people with hope and gives them a way to connect to God, seek comfort and guidance, and find inner peace. Prayer is also a form of meditation or self-reflection and can be done quietly, or out loud. Prayer allows people to talk to a higher power or the deity they believe in, to worship the concept of a God, and to further develop their relationship with a higher power or with God. Prayer is the key way people can develop this relationship with God and ask for help, favors, wishes, guidance, and grow closer to the higher power they seek to have a relationship with.

The spiritual perspective of prayer

Prayer has very strong roots within the belief systems of spirituality. Again, spirituality is the belief in something greater than ourselves and something of a spiritual nature. Spirituality doesn't always have to incorporate the concept of religion in it, but within religion you'll generally find elements of spirituality. Since spirituality is a broad concept of what is spiritual in nature, it's important to understand that the nature of prayer within spirituality is going to be the concept of talking to God or to the higher power that a person worships or praises or talks to and asks guidance from.

Prayer is an opportunity to get closer to God just as it is within religion as well, however, within spirituality prayer is perceived as a means to worship and follow God or a higher power within the means of becoming a more spiritual person in general and attaining a greater closeness to God. Prayer then becomes a chance to deepen one's spirituality, seek guidance, and experience a meaningful connection with God.

Prayer is just as important in spirituality as it is in religion and there are many different ways to pray within spirituality as there are within the concept of religion as well. Prayer can bring a sense of a spiritual or loving presence and alignment with God and an immersion into a Universal consciousness. Prayer can also elicit feelings of gratitude, compassion, forgiveness, and hope, all of which are associated with healing and wellness. Prayer can have immense healing benefits and capacities and is an integral part of spirituality and being a more spiritual person.

The religious perspective of prayer

Prayer is an extremely important part of religious practice and belief. Prayer is the wonderful manner by which a human is able to communicate with God and talk to Him in various forms and it is the way upon which people worship and give praise and thanks to God for the many blessings bestowed on them by Him.

Prayer is what nurtures obedience and patience and it allows the good in us to come forth, and lets us desire the concepts of obedience, grace, patience etc. We cannot gain the key aspects of knowledge, higher wisdom and truth unless we align with God the Creator in prayer.

Prayer practices within specific religions do vary in a huge way. In Islam, prayer is about specific physical postures and actually prostrating to the ground while reciting verses from the Quran the Holy book of Islam. In Buddhism, prayer can be completely different than this. It may involve meditation, deep reflection, and chanting.

Within Christianity, prayer is a way to communicate with God. It can take on the form of personal prayers, communal prayers or reciting specific prayers. Christians, just like Muslims might pray for different things such as forgiveness, strength, love, guidance etc. Prayer is especially perceived as a way to deepen one's relationship with God and seek His will. There are also many denominations within Christianity and different belief systems and ways of prayer within each denomination and belief system.

Types Of Prayer

There are a plethora of ways a person can pray and bow generously to God, their God or creator, a higher power or deity. There are numerous ways a person can utilize the concept of prayer and within various religious you'll also find different methods of prayer that worshippers utilize. There are many types of prayer out there and ways to worship God and prayer is the ultimate form of being able to speak with or talk to God in some way. Here are just a few methods that people do undertake when it comes to prayer and worship.

It is essential that people follow or combine different methods of prayer in order to be able to effectively communicate with God or the deity they worship and to get the best results and to receive the most of the prayer sessions they do have.

Worship/adoration

There are many ways a person can pray through worship and one can be through the power of song. Song is a very effective way to worship and adore and pray to God or the deity someone follows.

Thanksgiving

Giving thanks is a very special and important part of prayer and aspect to praying. It's important to always be in a state of feeling grateful for all the things that a person possesses and what has been given to someone or for the material possessions they do have.

It is important to constantly be thankful for all the wonderful things you do have and any capability you do possess as well. Being in a constant state of thanks and being grateful are effective ways of being able to pray.

Intercessory Prayer

This is when someone stands in the middle and supplicates for a person who doesn't have the ability or means to be able to pray for themselves. Sometimes a person can't always pray for themselves, so this kind of prayer will have to be done.

Fasting

Fasting is a very important way that a person can worship God or pray in some form. It is the withholding of food, water, drink etc, for specific periods of time as a means to worship God or to do for the cause or sake of God or a request made by God within a religion of people for a certain cause.

Fasting can be found in many religions and in the religion of Islam, there is a very special time when followers of the religion are asked to fast for an entire month from sunrise to sunset and it is called the month of Ramadan. This is a very important time for Muslims to withhold food and water and with it are supposed to come great rewards from God, and it is also a requirement that God has asked Muslims the followers of Islam to do twice a year.

Meditation

Meditation is a very popular, common and important way to be able to pray or to worship God through. Meditation is a beautiful and blessed path that people can take which involves quiet contemplation within the mind and deep thinking. It is a way for many people worldwide to be able to pray to or worship God in some form.

There are hundreds of forms of meditation out there and various ways of being able to meditate and to talk to God through this means.

Repentance prayers

Repentance prayers are exactly what they sound like they are. Repentance is important when approaching God and needs to be done very often when praying to God. It is important to repent and ask for forgiveness often and to confess to God any issues you're having or any sins you've committed. This is a way of getting closer to God as well and allowing yourself to form some form of a bond with the one you worship or praise.

Scripture Prayers

If you follow a religion or a religious book, you're able to find scriptures within the book and use those scriptures to assist you with praying to God in some format. Scriptures from religious texts are a powerful source for allowing you to pray to God when it comes to being a better person overall, and becoming more religious and spiritual in general.

The spiritual mind is one that is gifted with the beauty and the blessings of spiritual insight and one that is free and that has gotten rid of the ego completely. Our spiritual mind is one that is free of any blemishes. Spiritual transformation takes place when the soul is ready for growth and it's time to awaken and advance to the next level spiritually and to bring someone's spiritual gifts forth and use them to enhance a person's life and soul growth.

Transformation is a beautiful, wonderful gift that is given to the enlightened individual once they have achieved a specific level of awakening and growth from within and they have turned into a souled creation that is full of love, awakening and bliss energy. Once a person has mastered this level of soul growth, they are ready for any higher phases of spiritual awakening to take place and to grow even further and advance within the realms of good, their higher self, love and light.

www.ingramcontent.com/pod-product-compliance
Lightning Source LLC
LaVergne TN
LVHW020440070526
838199LV00063B/4796